F.F

Break Through Limitati...

Tap into Truth, Live Your Purpose.

Rachel Jenkins

First edition published in paperback in 2018 by Pure Energy Plus Ltd.

ISBN 978 1 5272 3439 0

Pure Energy Plus Ltd.
1a Abbey Terrace
Llandeilo
Carmarthenshire
SA19 6BD
Wales, UK

www.racheljenkins.online

"Life expectancy is not about how long you live, it is about the quality of your life in any given moment [...] If you do not look after your body, you will have nowhere to live"

Sir Paul McKenna

Gratitude

To all my family and friends who quietly support me in their own ways; trusting in who I am, what I do, and leaving me to freely get on with it.

To **Amber**: Thank you for all that you are, all that you have been, all that you are becoming and of course, for taking the back-cover photo for this book.

To my clients, past, present and future: From my heart, *you* are my inspiration. Thank you.

For helping me bring my work to you:

Brigit Thurston (Digital support), **Sarah MacDonald** (admin), **Raluca Comanaescu,** (My 'virtual' backbone) **Paul Ramsden,** (my web-guy,**) Nicky Hoddinott and Amanda Short,** (all online necessities).

To **Sophie Oliver, Shion Buschner and Hanna Azevedo** (nee Hedger) my beautifully dedicated *Rise & Shine* Support Team.

Niamh Kromo, my motivational catalyst: thank you. **Philippa Davies** for her 'best-selling' wisdom and support.

To **Vanessa Moss**, my Organic Lead Generation Coach: What a catalyst, power house and support you have been to me. Thank you for everything Vanessa.

Cherie Magee, my editor: Looking forward to the interviews where we describe how we put this book together in its final month of creation! (haha!) What an extraordinary experience this has been. Thank you so much for helping to ensure that everyone reading my words has the best chance of understanding what I mean (so that it can also help them in a profound way too!)

Chris Howard, thanks for your mentor (and friend)ship, alongside **Megan Black,** (his right-hand support).**Daniel Latto,** for all your great business advice. **Jo Stevens** for all your help and support. To **Mazatos Taverna** in Cyprus: What open hearted people; to the **Ogilvie Family** in the Old Coffee Shop, Maroni, Cyprus: If you have ever found yourself feeling challenged, miles away from home (and all that is familiar) then you will know what it feels like to unexpectedly find a place of safety and respite.

To **Sarah Strong,** my wonderful photographer, thank you **Richard Cotton,** for stepping in at the last minute to design this book cover. I love it.

For all the people who help to make life magical: **Eloise Bennett**, **Zlatko Kanda**, **Valentini Loizou, Susan Rudd, Linda Sparks** and **Conor O'Sullivan** (thank you for your TREPANIC music!), **Leah Robinson** (Nee Marshall), **Monique & Mike Saunders**, **Deborah Lewis** (Sea swimming buddy).

To *everyone*- I am unable to mention all names here right now, but you are probably within the book- and you know who you are- so I truly hope you know how much your support means to me. Some of you have been my teachers in more ways than one. Some of those lessons have been painful, but to anyone that I have ever hurt in anyway, I am sorry, please forgive me. To anyone who feels they have ever hurt me in some way, either with intent or by accident, I forgive you.

Know, that all is okay and now that I am FREE again, life is good and just as it is supposed to be.

~ Rachel

Contents

Foreword

In this life, sometimes it feels like people let you down in all sorts of ways. Some of them stay too long or leave too soon, maybe they try to change you (or bring you down) when you disagree with their opinions or behaviours. The reality is we all have times in our lives when we feel very unsupported and alone. However, it is during these times where we have the chance to realise that we mustn't rely on anyone for our joy – it isn't theirs to give or take away- unless of course, we *choose* to adopt their words and actions as something that defines our experience. But, where do we place our power then? You see, in our quest to belong, we forget that 'belongings' are owned, and it is perhaps no coincidence that the word 'longing' is hidden therein.

The truth is, we are never going to find (or satisfy) ourselves 'out there' in society; even with the best intentions, all we will find is *other* people's desires, wishes and dreams for us, or roles to fit into and comply with. Slowly but surely, we will forget who we came here to be. If we look to the world for answers - instead of within- we leave our own treasures to be found *last*, and then we wonder why we feel as if there is something missing. Well, of course there is: we haven't been there for ourselves, it is *us* who have not shown up, *we* have been missing. We were looking for someone 'better' for the job to make us happy – what message does this send to our self- worth? In this state of personal neglect, it is no time at all before we get anxious or depressed; defined by the negative thought that we mustn't be worthy of true joy, because we are not feeling it fully. We haven't been owning it.

However, it's time to realise that while you might be fretting over everything that isn't working for you; one thing *always* is– your heart. It spends all of its time incessantly beating to keep you full of life, and you didn't even ask it to. It was awake before you'd ever even formed a thought and so you see, whatever autonomous magic lives in your heart – *it's all for you*. When you were worrying about what everyone else would think or want, its only job was to keep safe the unique importance of *your* life. So, if you are your heart's only priority, when are you going to start listening to what it really wants you to *know* about yourself? When are you going to support *yourself* and start using the magnificent life you've been given?

What Rachel offers you in this book is something really simple and honest, and yet it is the only path home; a doorway back into who you really are inside. In today's society of external noise, distraction and instant information, we all could use a quiet place to access our forgotten wisdom, and tune back into what really matters. Perhaps you have been led away from your true desires, or have been putting everybody else ahead of your own needs; maybe you've lived the illusion that selflessness means being last. However, if you want to genuinely help anyone, you can only do so from a place of internal freedom first. Otherwise, you are just leading others into the same darkness and illusion that you refuse to emerge from. You need to pull away from the need to be liked, to be accepted or swayed from your own internal compass, and you need to *give into yourself,* just as Rachel has done to discover and share her truth. If there is one thing that Rachel's book will help you understand, it is that having true courage to face yourself (exactly as you are) pays unlimited mental, physical, emotional and spiritual dividends, beyond anything you can ever imagine.

Is it sometimes tough to do? *Yes.*

Does it mean following through on new decisions that might not always suit everyone? *Yes.*

Could you lose some people that aren't here for your highest good? *Most likely.*

But that is what courage is and Rachel has it in bundles. Not everything beautiful is easy and every rose comes with thorns, but it doesn't have to be complicated. Rachel has the resolve to sit with herself every day, and listen to the feelings generated by her heart. She takes one day at a time, appreciates what she has been given and acts on her intuition with strength, clarity and bravery. She knows that by going into her own heart for true love, it will never let her down or lead her astray, and that if it works for her, it will work for you. You just have to be willing to take responsibility for your own joy and begin the process of stripping yourself from every fear that's been holding you back.

Throughout this book, you will learn that if you tap into the part of you that never lies, (even when everything on the outside seems to), you can trust again. No matter what has happened to you, Rachel will show that the sunshine *always* follows the rain, so long as you prepare for the storm and have total knowing that it will pass. Even if she has an 'off' day, she is gentle with herself because no outcome is more perfect than the consistent practise of self-love.

I'm also privileged to know Rachel outside of work, and not only has she got the most heart-warming laugh, but she is also a lioness of a mother. Whether or not she is 'liked' in the moment, she will never seek the 'quick fix' to avoid pain, instead she stays loyal to the bigger picture so that she can be the example she wants to teach her daughter, not just talk about it. Anyone can advise or mentor, but the truest leaders are the ones who reach out their hands, roll up their sleeves and say, 'Come on, let's walk this path together.' Rachel's disciplined daily practise means that she is now easily able to follow through on decisions that change lives, breed new results and help to express her profound gifts to the world. I think it is time you did the same, and allowed yourself to claim your power back, one day of self-investigation at a time. If you want to believe in true love, then I promise you will find it only when you truly love yourself. True love is brave enough to say 'no' to things that don't feel 'true' for you. Every time you get a nudge saying, 'I know I have to do this'... that's true love. That is your internal guidance switching on and begging you to listen, and every time you don't – one way or another – you will experience suffering.

When I was a kid, I used to watch the X-Files, a show about alien life and all kinds of weird and wonderful possibilities. Their catchphrase was, 'The truth is out there'. Today, Rachel is going to show you that it is *not.* If you want the truth, you must go in the opposite direction that you have been taught... go inside *yourself* and find it. It will be buried, it will be scary and honouring it might mean getting up and leaving a situation that up until now, you have been too afraid to walk out on. But there is no happy ending in living a lie, and every time you avoid doing what *feels* right, the true you is being silenced and cast aside. Take Rachel's hand and walk the path into a life that has *your* hopes and dreams at the very centre of it. That is where you will find freedom.

Cherie Magee

(Psychological Wellness Expert & Editor)

Introduction

Most people who meet me for the first time, have no idea of the level of vulnerability that I used to experience and how affected I was by it. That's because today: happiness, energy, vibrancy and vitality are more often than not, my norms. I now do what I love most days. It's an especially nourishing existence teaching others how to get there and experience this too. Earlier this year, a dear friend and highly respected coach, sat me down one day and said:

"People need to understand and meet the *vulnerable* you. Because that's how you can help them the most."

I hadn't realised how important it was until that moment. She was right. Many people around the world- who have already experienced my *Rise and Shine* Meditation and Coaching programmes- usually only witness the fun, empowered, inspiring side of me.

This wasn't always me. I had to do the inner work during highly distressing and challenging periods in my life to find the light which at times, felt like a very, very long dark tunnel.

Some of the challenges I faced in my adult life have been a result of negatively charged emotional experiences, buried in my subconscious since child- hood. They only came to light in my thirties, when part of me sought understanding and closure. It has been enlightening.

In this book, I hadn't really wanted to "go there", to share my personal challenges and vulnerability, but I knew there would be profound significance in sharing my journey with others. Every time I speak my truth about how vulnerable, lonely and desperate I was in my past, it helps someone else to rapidly recognise and move through their own challenges with more ease and grace. I wish to take you to a place where new perspectives can be born, balance can be discovered, and daily peace can return.

This is my first book, it feels very exciting, even though it hasn't turned out as I thought it would. I have laughed and cried as I re-opened old experiences, but I am by no means a qualified author, if there is such a thing. I have simply written a book that I felt called to write, and when you read the whole book, you will understand what I mean.

Unexpectedly, I planned for this book to teach you how to:

- overcome the restless mind everyday
- connect with inner truth and live by it in a powerfully positive way
- overcome overwhelm, fear, and burnout
- feel amazing and be the master creator in your life

That's because many people all over the world, are already enjoying these results after using my *Rise & Shine* models. However, during the book process, I have had to let go of my initial plan and trust that what resulted in the end was much more in line with my truth:

- It lets you into my vulnerability

- My fears
- My anger
- My confusion
- My past
- My lowest moments

It's about the journey that I travelled to get me here: a place where I can enjoy all the simple things in life again, after releasing myself from the shackles of my mind. A place where I can create, from a space of FREEDOM.

In getting here, I have had to dig deep and face things about MYSELF, to move through some seriously challenging times. I still don't always get it right, even now, years later. It's because I'm human and I'm still learning too.

We are here to experience, to let go, to love, to live.

In my experience it takes work to live a highly evolved, enlightened and spiritual life – which to me simply means *living in the heart.* When life throws me challenges, I find myself meeting myself, and I welcome the woman I meet every time.

Others may not like what they see in me, especially if they have not resolved the things in themselves that I reflect, or if there is no level of mutual experience to connect with. That's OK. This book is only about speaking my truth. It's about having the courage and conviction to trust why I am here writing these words to you.

You may not like or agree with anything that I write. That's fine because this is only my experience. *F.R.E.E.D.O.M.* provides the autobiographical context as to why I dedicated the last decade to creating and evolving my *Rise and Shine* models, for both adults and children. My story is designed to inspire you to find peace. To let you know that you can find yourself and your centre when no-one else truly understands what is happening in your mind and life. It's about having the courage to let go and accept- to move on regardless. To love yourself enough to say "No" (or "Yes" depending on the situation). I have learnt that whatever others think of you is their business and it just does not matter.

This book exists to help you understand that you're in charge of your mind, and therefore the level of freedom that you experience in your life on a moment to moment basis. When you truly learn how to overcome the restless mind, access the wisdom of the heart and navigate yourself through fear, you can be the leader of your own life. My wish is to inspire you to live in alignment with YOUR truth, regardless of your age, gender, race, religious, spiritual or sexual inclination. Your truth is your truth.

Some of what I say may cause discomfort but THANK YOU for being here, it's just the beginning.

Rachel

P.S. I would LOVE to hear from you, if my words have helped you in some way.

Chapter 1 - Being 'OK' with Uncertainty

1.1 - Feeling Uncomfortable is Part of The Process

I'm happy and centred each morning and night these days, but the fact is: I didn't just wake up like this randomly–I had to face all my fears and work towards my own internal freedom with self-discipline and courage. I had to follow my heart with blind faith and trust, to make some really tough decisions that caused me a lot of initial suffering. Change can be painful and frightening, even when you know deep down, it is what you really need to be deeply happy. So often, we stay stuck in situations that no longer serve us because we are afraid to rock the boat. The consequence is mental anguish or physical illness and in March 2010, after ignoring all the warning signs that I hadn't been living my truth, I finally had a nervous breakdown.

You see, for a long time I'd been fighting the truth that my marriage wasn't working anymore, though parts of me just hadn't been prepared to accept it. I was mentally exhausted, in pain and filled with confusion as to what to do next, even though my heart was telling me it was time to leave. We had a young daughter, a life, a joint business; from the outside, it probably looked like we were 'OK', and maybe somehow, I had told myself the same thing. One day, I found myself staring at my wedding ring on the kitchen counter with a letter that I had written to my husband, telling him I wanted to separate. I asked for forgiveness, and yet in some ways, I didn't even know what I was sorry for, because all I wanted was to be happy, and being there unhappy wasn't helping anyone. The problem was that I was so afraid of this change, that it ended up being a whole year before I finally made the decision and left for good.

You see, nothing had been the same since I returned from London: I had been attending an intensive six-month leadership programme two years prior and since the event, my whole outlook on life had changed. Slowly, it had dawned on me who I was, who I wanted to become and what I really wanted in this life, and I realised I really wasn't living it. I wasn't happy in my marriage, no matter how hard I tried to make it so, and I also felt that I had skills and beliefs that no one- even my husband- could recognise or appreciate. During my time in London, I had felt something profound; I didn't want to go home, because I didn't want to lose myself back in that life where I was gradually forgetting who I was and what I had to do. The people that were at the event were like-minded and they had woken up to their own gifts, they seemed to be cracking on with everything they wanted to achieve and there was I, holding myself back for the sake of my marriage. I wanted to make a difference to the world, something beyond what I had been doing up until that point.

After months of training and crewing as a coach, I began to know what I wanted to do and how to do it; I had felt it, I 'got' it. But when I returned home, just as I had feared, my dreams began to slip away again. I felt totally isolated because I was living in Wales at the time. It was where my family, home and seasonal beach business were based and almost no one even spoke my language. It was a sign in some respects because that is exactly how I felt metaphorically, no one really 'got' who I was there, they didn't speak or think like me and I was so frustrated that I had chosen to be this alone. It is especially ironic to feel separated from society because by that time, I had started to develop this gift for intuitively *feeling* people, it became almost a curse to empathise with people so deeply and as I'll explain later, I was searching for a way to turn it off and trying to focus a bit more on myself.

I eventually understood that before I really helped people, I had internal work to do and that possibly I had manifested a relationship that was a direct reflection of the unhappiness that lay dormant within me. For example, in the Summer of 2008, I had attended the first part of Christopher Howard's Leadership Programme in London and received my training in Neurolinguistics. I'd learnt the science of how the mind works; how the subconscious stores our emotions, including the repressed ones (the ones that we don't remember but drive our experience) and how those memories actually get stored in our DNA. The problem is we don't know what we don't know, because the subconscious hides it from us to keep us safe from pain. When we were hurt as a child, those emotions- if unresolved – get stored and give our actions an emotional meaning. Therefore, two people can see the exact same event and place different meanings on it. One person's pain and perception may not exist in another, because what something means is unique to each person. We only see the world through our *own* lens.

I knew all this and yet had failed up until the breakdown to recognise that there was trauma inside *me*, sitting dormant for decades, manifesting dissatisfaction, inhibiting joy and leaving me stuck in an endless loop of sitting in the shadow of my true potential, pleasing other people and hoping it would change. I knew however that only I could change it. To most people, I was happily married and in some surface level ways – I was. Underneath it all, my soul felt unfulfilled and stuck in the past, so London showed me the contrast of what could be truly happy and free for me (compared to the life I was currently living, which satisfied my mind to a degree but no further). For a few years I had the creeping suspicion that under my smiles, my marriage had been -to an extent- a lie. The soul inside wanted more, it knew I was to do something *more* than what I had created up until now. I realised there was a lack and that I was being reliant on something external to make it better. In this case, it was my marriage and in 2004, it had been my addiction to cigarettes. Strangely, in January of that year, I had finally got that I was 'addicted' to something outside of myself for relief and overnight, I had quit with no symptoms. Despite laughing about how foolish I had been then, and even though I never returned to smoking, I noticed that I had somehow created a new addiction to make myself happy from something 'out there': my husband. But how was I going to quit this time?

To find the answer, I did what I do best: I meditated on it. Should I stay? Was I crazy to leave? Should I listen to that voice inside of me that felt it was time, or stick it out? Quitting smoking was a walk in the park compared to this; this was different, it was deep. I honestly felt like I was going mad. Do you remember a time where you felt completely uncertain about where to go next, when you know something feels bad, but the consequences could easily end up feeling bad anyway? It is frightening, especially when there is no road map away from the comfortable territory you have been on for years. This decision was not only going to affect my life but also my daughter Amber, and of course, my husband. How would he react? Honestly, I didn't want my truth to cause them any pain. I'm sure they had already been subjected to enough pain given that my unhappiness had not been well hidden over the last few years, but the whisperings of my heart told me that something was not as it should be. How do you explain that to people who think of this as whacky mumbo-jumbo? Yet, with every inch of my being, I had to listen. It was the real 'me' talking, and as I sat on that yoga mat, tuning into myself, trying to find peace of mind or even an answer, I knew I wouldn't hear the easy option or what I wanted to hear. I got the answer loud and clear: *I had to leave.*

Every day thereafter that I found myself stuck in indecision of *how* to leave, I suffered incredibly, and just so you know how hard it is to make such a decision, I remind you that it took me one full year to finally act. On November 11, 2011, I decided enough was enough and it didn't come from inside this time: I returned home to a note from my six-year old daughter asking to go to boarding school to 'get some peace and quiet'. My heart was broken, I didn't realise that my unhappiness had caused enough argument in the house to nearly drive her away. This is the result of procrastination of what you *know* inside is right. Thinking that staying and feeling bad is of benefit to your child never works and I know that now. Seeing that note made me jump straight into doing the right thing finally. Everyone had had enough of the lie. It only took a split second, and suddenly I was thinking of where I would live, how I would survive because I had shut down my coaching business due to the nervous breakdown, so I hadn't been getting my usual income. I wasn't ready for this, I wasn't even recovered – but who is? All uncertainty vanished in that moment of worrying about what my daughter was seeing and experiencing – change needed to happen... *now*. A voice in my head said, 'pick up your yoga mat and go', it couldn't have been any clearer. This time I listened and walked out the door.

I needed to create some space to breathe in the first instance and figure it out from there. I was suffocating in my own home. I could not function and so this would be good for all of us in the long run. We lived a stone's throw away from my parent's farm, in the same village, so I asked my mother if I could rent their holiday cottage for a few weeks while I gathered my thoughts and worked out what to do next. What was important to me, was finding a way to stay near Amber's father so we could have contact, and be close to her school, my family and our beach business (a mile and a half down the road). At that point, I could not see further than that. I had been battling with myself for so long about finally making the decision and taking the action to leave that now, in doing so, there was suddenly a huge sense of relief but also, a void.

I knew that to get through this period, I had to feel full trust in my decision and accept that what I had just done was the best decision for all of us, even though I did not fully understand the path. It took some courage and self-belief, but I drowned out every voice that was holding me back and just listened to my inner guidance that it would all work out.

I remember standing outside the cottage that my parents owned, which was a fifty-metre walk from my marital home, telling my daughter (with the most integrity I could muster), 'Amber, we are not going to be living with Daddy anymore.' To which she responded- because I now realise children *need* truth- 'That's OK Mummy, it's not about me, is it? Let's dance.'

As you can probably imagine, that's the last thing I thought would come out of her mouth. I felt her relief... and I felt mine... so that's what we did. We danced like maniacs until all the concrete blocks fell away from my shoulders. I was blown away by her ability to overcome drama and pain and gain something beautiful from the truth. She was six and I was a grown woman and it had taken me until that point to realise what I should have acted on, a year earlier. Cut loose and dance, it is why we are here.

However, that night, even with her beautiful example, I couldn't sleep. My head was in knots, my neck seized up again, I felt overcome with pain and worry. As I lay there, I tried to recall the conference that I had attended with my friend Dawn in London called 'You Can Do It' by Louise Hay, (I'd only met her once, but I was intensely grateful for the meeting) and a question from that seminar came to mind:

'What can you do this month that is going to make the biggest difference to the quality of your life?'

Then I had a strange simplistic thought, 'From now on, go to bed at 10pm and get up at six am.'

It sounded too easy, but that is exactly what I did. Six am became five am because I naturally woke up at that time and suddenly, I had a pattern. I began to feel calm, organised. I started to experience deep peace, clarity and understanding that what I needed was to honour my deepest, simplest voice. In a time of chaos, what more can you ask for? I had spent so long trying to fix the outside; not knowing what to do, how I could make everyone happy and manage their pain, that I had forgotten how to do what I did when I stopped smoking: just stop.

You can do this too if you take some time to be you, develop a system that makes you feel regular again, forge a new path and stick to it. It is all about the action. After I did this regular focusing a few days after walking out of my marriage, something new happened- something profound- and it increased the faith in me that my decision had been correct: I started to fully believe in myself.

In that disciplined space of sitting with myself at a certain time in the morning and a regular time at night, the answers came. I was given instructions on what to do and I promise you, they came from nowhere. The words just kept coming, effortlessly and I started to channel energies I'd never heard of before called 'Melchizedek' and 'Joseph of Arimathea'. Naturally, I googled them out of curiosity and realised that they were significant people in the bible. From these inner channellings, and with Louise Hay's seminar in mind, (that dis-ease is created from emotions), I started a new journey... I was coming back to myself, I wasn't running away. I knew my new inner guides would lead me to the answer of who I really was, why I had left and ultimately how I would begin to finally face myself.

1.2 - Facing Yourself is The First Step to Freedom

When I first left, it felt right but I also felt guilty for 'running away' at the start. In facing how I was truly feeling, I released the guilt (from what appeared to be 'running away' from my problems), by realising I wasn't trying to escape; it was me coming back to *myself*. In fact, I had one question that came to me anytime I felt like I would just run back to safety; one that I now wish to ask you:

'How much *pain* are your prepared to accept in your life?'

I decided that I didn't want to accept any more pain, at least not recycled pain over and over that never seemed to move me forward. At least if leaving caused me pain, it was *new* pain; pain from change, from the fear of the unknown and from listening to myself, rather than pain of being stuck in old patterns just for the sake of it. In fact, I began to ask myself as many simple, quality questions as I could to stay determined. In 2008, during Christopher Howard's Leadership course, one of the things he advised stuck with me:

"The quality of your life is determined by the questions you ask yourself".

You see, something magical happens when you change the quality of your questions. Instead of my old habit of asking, 'Why me?' or 'How did I get here?' I had started to ask questions that would open up space for a positive solution. Do you know what happens when you start asking yourself questions about yourself instead of the environment or people out there, that you feel are to blame for your unhappiness? You get deeper, better answers, that's what happens. Unfortunately, sometimes the answers might be quite challenging to hear. The reason for this is that we are all exceptional *liars*. Did you know that we are all really good at lying? Yes, lying. That includes you and me and most of the time, we have created so many stories for ourselves to keep us from pain that we don't even realise what we *think* we want or feel mightn't be true. I'll give you an example:

Shortly after I had physically left my marital home, a very good friend of mine asked me the usual question; if I was 'okay'. I said what many of us say in times like these, "Yes I'm fine!". But friends see what you don't want to and a few weeks later, he called me on it. He said, "You've got that pretty well honed, haven't you?" I was confused and wondered what he meant by that. He added, "You've convinced yourself that you are okay, when clearly you are not". I was stopped in my tracks. The truth was, I wasn't lying to him, I really thought I was doing fine, given the circumstances; I had a grasp on everything and all was OK, right? The reality was that I hadn't lied to anyone, I had lied to *myself* and when he spotted it, I realised that I was operating not from the truth of how I was really feeling, but pulling out my "norm" or my "coping mechanism", which was to cover up my real feelings, and he was right, I'd really gotten good at it. I mean, let's face it, I had left my home when I was never going to feel ready for that. I'd been miserable at home because I felt isolated and unhappy in my marriage, and equally sad because I had no future plan. I was truly lost and all because I had listened to my gut. Was this the freedom I had wanted? It didn't feel that way. The alternative was equally painful, so I wasn't about to run back, it was against the tiny voice inside. I had to care for our daughter and the truest way to do that was to get myself back together, start again and be happy for her sake. I realised I would have to get back to coaching, earn more money and gain some financial security before I did anything else. However, I was in no shape to coach others through their challenges when I was still in recovery from my own nervous breakdown and subsequent departure from my family home and structure. All these thoughts crashed in on me like a tidal wave when my friend told me that he could *see* I was unhappy, and then all my real feelings and worries came over me so fast that I thought I might just drown in them. My safety net had gone. How was I going to keep trusting that everything would work out?

Suddenly, I pictured myself eating ice-cream on the beach and remembered back to the situation surrounding the ice-cream and organic snacks business that my husband and I had set up back in April 2003, when the story returned to me:

We had renovated an ice-cream van just before we had gotten married and had enjoyed the ease of running a small business, which essentially helped put smiles on many faces. Adults and children alike had initially appeared wide eyed and excited at the counter, searching for their favourite ice-cream flavour. It was delightful, very easy to do and lots of fun. People would come down to the beach and just keep appearing every day. However, we had a problem: some locals would not accept the fact that the land was privately owned by my family. You see, when my grandfather had returned from World War I, his life changing experience made him appreciate what really matters in life. We recall him saying that "some things in life should be free" and his idea was that it was particularly important for the elderly and children to have access to the beach on our land, at no cost.

As time passed though, things changed. The protective sea wall had come to the end of its life, and the council planned to remove it. This meant that the land adjacent to the beach (which enabled access and car parking) would be flooded in the near future, and cottages there would be threatened too. I became heavily involved in seeking solutions to establish how to protect the land and because of this, the spotlight was back on the land at the beach, our ownership and our family. This land had been open for anyone to park and enjoy the beauty and magic of a stunning bay and beach, under our family's custodianship since 1915. Thousands and thousands of visitors along with our local community had freely enjoyed access to this beautiful beach, in alignment with my grandfather's wishes for many years. However, with an imminent change in coastal management policy, the sea wall was about to come down. This brought up many things for many people.

Eventually, instead of happy faces appearing at our simple, welcoming, homely beach business, complaint after complaint would be heard about one thing or another to do with the beach access. The joy of overseeing a sweet business that provided a service to many and helped put smiles on faces, was no longer able to be what it was. The beach had come a point of contention and the ice-cream business had too. With the background politics rearing its ugly head about what would happen to the future access at the beach, my husband and I had gotten tired of being on the front end of receiving and dealing with it. The fun and joy had vanished. The ice-cream business had therefore come to the end of its natural life for me in many ways, due to circumstances that were out of my control and there was nothing I could do about it, because like leaving my marriage, it was out of my hands. I had no choice but to let go of what wasn't working.

The reason why that story of our business had come into my head became clear. Back then, I had been struggling to decide if I should let go or fight the situation, with ten thousand thoughts in my head of what to actually do. But only in silence, when I'd let go of the whole logic, did the answer come; it was like a tiny whisper in my ear and it almost seemed too simple: "Let nature take its course". Back then, I trusted this intuition and stopped trying to co-ordinate a holistic solution for the future of access to the beach that would meet everybody's needs. I'd already set up all sorts of meetings with Pembrokeshire County Council, (our community Council), the National Park, the National Trust, Water Based Activity Provider Businesses, Pembrokeshire Outdoor Charter, geologists, and the list goes on. It was impossible and exhausting. Everyone seemed to have different agendas and it was all being done on my time and that of my family's.

I finally trusted and decided that you cannot fight nature. If the sea was going to come in, it was going to come in, and my life purpose was not to be the person who was running themselves ragged, trying to find a positive solution that everyone was happy with. It seemed I had been setting myself up for failure in trying to do the right thing by everybody. I got to the point that I was absolutely exhausted just by thinking about the beach or the ice-cream business and I did not want to be there anymore. It was no longer a source of joy for me. It was time to let go of the beach, the ice-cream business and follow my true calling: to re-start my coaching practise, and awaken others to the truth of what is really important in life. I wanted to help them actualise that in their lifetimes.

I am telling you all this for one reason only, and it is one of the reasons why most people *don't* follow their guts:

I usually receive answers that are **NOT** the easy course of action to take. Sometimes, they go against everything I think I should do.

Because the answers that come to us can be painful, even scary, most people shut that little voice of truth out and continue in their cycles of rehashed pain. My advice is that it *is* scary, and it is hard to listen because it is not emotionally easy to follow blindly what you *feel*, instead of what you logically think. If you are to live your true purpose however, you simply must deeply listen to yourself. It is what you really need, even if it is not what you want in that moment. The only way to let go of pain is to hand it over to whatever it is you believe in; call it God, source, space, the universe-the label doesn't matter- what matters is that you feel looked after and safe in following the guidance that emerges.

For example, when I do my daily meditative practise, I say this:

"I ask that all my thoughts, words and deeds be directed by source for the highest good of all under the Law of Grace".

I start with this intention *before* I ask any question because it allows me to trust that any answers I receive are for my highest good, and so it never feels like a mistake at the deepest level. This is really facing yourself or in short- *trusting yourself fully*- and listening to your gut above all else, even during the most difficult decisions.

Here is the meditative pattern I use that is fairly simple but absolutely works to help solve difficult 'cross-road' moments:

6 DAILY MEDITATION GUIDANCE STEPS

1. Ask yourself simple but high-quality questions (with the view of finding a practical solution)
2. Listen to the answers as if they are wise Gods that are there to help you
3. Ask for absolute clarity and certainty beyond measure (in the form of signs or words etc.) and expect it to come.
4. Trust yourself to follow the course of action which will reveal itself and see it as necessary action.
5. Take *swift* action on the directions that come from deep within. If you wait too long, you'll chicken out and not do anything. (Remember, I took a year to act and follow my own guidance on my relationship, and all that happened is I did it anyway, felt pain anyway and had a year's delay!)
6. Set your intention to experience feelings of deep peace, bliss and joy during the process of facing the truth. Remind yourself that your deepest self would never advise anything that would harm you – feel good about that.

You will discover as you read further in my story, that there are many more questions I ask myself, as I face myself EVERY DAY. These questions create not only a feeling of freedom in that moment, but also empower me to express and act in a way that feels authentically aligned with myself. That is *freedom* that no one can give me, it's already in there.

Now, one of the questions I get asked a lot is: But how do I know *which* truth is the truth? There are many voices in our head all day, so it is hard to know which one the 'real' voice is – the one that comes from the heart and soul.

How can you know if you are lying to yourself?

Well, in general, there are ways to find out if you are really living your truth. The biggest sign, (and the most obvious one) is found when you stand in the mirror. Can you look at yourself and find reasons to feel happy, grateful and joyful about what you see? If not, there's work to do, because you are *not* in alignment. Your truest self is *happiness*, it is the most natural way to be. Of course, there are other signs and questions you can ask yourself to find out where you are at:

- Do you complain about yourself?
- Do you complain about another person?
- Do you stay in a job that does not fulfil you, but you have convinced yourself that you "need to stay there"?

I had a job like that once, in fact, now that I look at it, I stayed about three years longer than I should have – just another self-inflicted suffering caused by me *not* following my heart and trying to satisfy too many other objectives! For example, when my husband and I moved back to my home county Pembrokeshire in 1999 (before we were married) we wanted to set up a music events company, and so we were pointed to a small business training day. We attended, and I was so inspired by Mike Hopkins, our trainer (and owner of a local Management Training company), that a few days later, I decided to approach him and ask if his business needed any extra marketing help. I imagined that this role would be good for me part-time because Matt and I were in the developmental stages of our business, and the extra money always helped. Moving back to my home village, in rural Wales, to set up a music events company was no small task, especially when the events I intended to run were a good three hours' drive away – in Bristol. We were driving back and forward to Bristol for late night gigs, where my husband would be DJing or where we would be promoting or running one of our events. Music had always lit me up and I felt passionate about it; it was just brilliant, so much fun.

My passion however for the marketing role began to vanish. I was feeling stuck from Monday to Thursday, or Tuesday to Friday, sitting in a remote office in West Wales, feeling unfulfilled and bored. Don't get me wrong, I was speaking to lovely people all over the country about their training needs in the corporate world, understanding more about what they needed, and feeding this back to our consultants to help them develop and refine their programmes. But it just left me feeling flat, it didn't light me up the way the music and events industry did, that was all. It was the same thing, day in day out but it was safe. It meant that I could take risks in the infancy stages of my own business, because I was still receiving a steady income whilst developing it. Even though it was a logical approach to staying afloat, I knew it wasn't a good enough reason to stay in a job that was lowering my energy. My full potential was not being maximised in a role within that business and I am not sure if it could have been either.

I remember I was so bored that I once sneaked my pillow into work and slept under the desk when no one was looking. Is that really living or just surviving? This is what happens when you stay in a job for money. That's not the goal, that's not joy. Indeed, are you stuck inside a job or even a *relationship* that does not light up your heart and lift your spirits, just by thinking about that person? I think everyone deserves the 'butterflies'; the joyful feeling of just knowing you are coming home to 'the one' who 'gets' you more than anyone! But how can life open up space for that outcome, when you won't *first* let go of the wrong person? The truth is you should never feel 'wrong' when you are on the 'right' path, so if you are consistently:

- Feeling rubbish
- Not wanting to get out of bed with pure delight every day
- Not wanting to go to work
- Experiencing little joy
- Having no daily excitement
- Feeling no playfulness
- Lacking in energy
- Feeling frightened

- Feeling stuck
- Feeling depressed
- Feeling overwhelmed
- Feeling doubtful
- Feeling anxious
- Feeling out of balance
- Feeling unwell
- Grumpy
- Jealous
- Spiteful
- Restless
- Lacking in Focus
- Comparing yourself to others
- Experiencing co-dependency of any kind
- Having any addiction
- Giving your own power away to ANYONE else...

Then you are not facing yourself and living your truth!

I know because I have - at different times- experienced *all* these moments of doubt and despair. I have stayed stuck for the safety of money and for the safety of routine but basically, if you are not living in a state of flow for most of the time, something is *not* in harmony inside of you!

Can you see yet where I am going with this? I strongly believe that when we are doing anything that takes us out of our state of flow, something isn't going to your soul's plan. Being in a place of flow feels so deeply enriching that nothing outside of you can touch those feelings of deep peace and bliss, because they are being generated from *within*. From this space, you need zero external validation because you know without doubt that you are wholesome and loved beyond measure, regardless of anyone else. In fact, when you are connected to your own heart, you exude an inner glow and confidence that cannot be replaced by anything 'worldly'. I understand that fear is a natural emotion but do not see it as the enemy, it is your opportunity to grow. Every time you feel the fear and *still* act in the direction of your inner wisdom, you're teaching yourself how safe you are in that wisdom.

You will know you have faced yourself, when you actually confront the lies you are telling yourself. It is time to be really happy, not just happy in the comfort zone. Outside of the comfort zone, a different space opens up where you realise you are a magnificent being. You make peace with yourself, you exist in a divine state of grace. True freedom has no boundaries; it is measured neither by time, nor money, or perceived 'success'. It's all inside. When you truly get this, nothing can touch you again. But for now, if any of the problems or negative feelings I have listed here-when you look in that mirror-feel *true* for you, (and you have faced this reality of how you are feeling) then I'm going to show you how important it is to overcome ego and not be afraid to ask for 'help'. After all, that is just another step for you towards courage and acceptance.

1.3 – Asking for Help is Brave

It's taken me quite some time to really "get" that asking for help is brave. If you are not feeling happy, who do you go to? If I remember back to my break-down, I'd say that if it wasn't for my amazing parents, I would have had a full 'melt-down'. I remember I was lying in my mother's best friend's house in 2010, I can't remember the month, but I remember how my head was feeling; it was pounding. At the time, I knew I couldn't be alone with these feelings anymore, and that I would need the courage to ask them if I could come home. Things were rock bottom and I did some 'crazy' things that in hindsight, I now know to be symptoms of my 'depression'. I'd smashed a crystal glass jug full of red wine all over the wall of my house – just missing my husband's head - (Sorry, Matt). He'd not long painted the wall either. In fact, I have no idea what the argument was about now, all the disagreements seemed to have merged into one, but I knew I was feeling really unwell. Mum and dad accepted what was happening and they took me to their house for some rest and recuperation. I optimistically thought that with a little time-out, I'd be okay in a couple of days, but this was <u>not</u> the case. The craziest thing happened one night (when I lay in bed at my parent's friend's house, where they had taken me for a change of scenery), I heard a voice from inside my head which said,

"Don't worry, you're going to wake up on the <u>other side</u> in a few minutes".

I will never forget that sentence, nor what happened next because I can recall it as vividly as if it was yesterday. I was all alone in the bedroom, and at the time I felt strangely peaceful. Suddenly, I felt like I was going to die. Like it was my *time*. I was unsure of how this feeling started, or why the voice had said that, but I just knew that something was going to happen, and I would be no more. My time was up here, and I had just a few minutes to accept it.

My response was:

"What have I done to deserve this?"

I was so confused as to why I absolutely felt in every cell of my body that I was going to die. I knew I had been feeling stressed, I was at my wits end, frustrated, confused, angry, and – at the time- trying to resolve a marriage that no longer felt full of fun, love or joy but how could I be lying here now, listening to a voice in my head that told me I had 'two minutes' to live? I just knew innately that was *it* and- in that very moment- I remember *accepting* it. I mean *totally* accepting it as fact. "Okay, so it's my time then". I said aloud. There was no logic or analysis necessary as to why this was happening anymore. I just made the decision to accept the situation and I said 'good bye' to everyone in my life, in my mind. No-one was there with me and I closed my eyes in full trust that I would not see anyone that I loved again; not my parents, my husband, siblings, my daughter who was five at the time, anyone. I had no time to think, it was quite an extraordinary experience. I remember distinctly that I felt no fear, no pain, I merely let go of everything that meant anything to me. For some reason, it just felt simple. I let go of everyone I loved. Nothing else mattered and I was awash with such a deep sense of peace. I said, “sorry” and “thank you” for my life and I fell into a deep sleep.

The next morning, to my astonishment, I woke up. The sun was shining through the curtains. I was alive, and everything had changed. I was feeling totally new, like I had been reborn. I got out of bed, filled with a new gratitude for life that I had never experienced. Words do not describe the depth of emotion that I felt when I saw my family. It was like looking through the eyes of a child with bright and beautiful awareness. I didn’t even really want to talk much, I just wanted to feel them, to *be* there. I seemed to be settling into a new realm of something, I didn’t know what. That wasn’t all, what had changed most of all was how I felt towards others; even my husband, who I had been lobbing things at a few days before. I just felt “nothing” when he appeared. No anger, no hatred, I was blank, even *happy* to see him when he arrived with our daughter. Of course, if that was the end, this book would be very short, and I would be floating on a cloud but as we all know, moments of enlightenment happen and then we realise there’s still a journey back to health that isn’t as easy as that. Like I said in the previous chapter, you must *face* all aspects of yourself before you are fully free. The feelings of peace had lasted for a few days and I am grateful for them, but something had been switched on by facing the idea of my own death; something inside me from the past had shifted and bubbled up to the surface to be looked at.

In the following week, I thought about all the things that had contributed to my final breakdown and I realised that a major factor had been something my friends (a couple) had disclosed to me. Obviously, they hadn't known the distress I was in and how overwhelmed I was when they talked to me about their problems, and so they shared some frightening details with me. While I cannot disclose it fully to you out of respect, the story was that their lives were being threatened by someone, and empathetic as I am, I hadn't been able to get it out of my head and had been feeling deeply worried about them. The peaceful feelings had allowed me to forget for a while but slowly the terror crept in. They had not gone to the police because they had been held back by fear. Something dark in me awoke in that moment, when I dwelled on their situation. A childhood memory emerged: I was about eleven years of age, when someone in the neighbourhood decided to threaten my family's lives. I remembered standing in the hallway of our home; the look on my mother's face as she put the phone down was terrifying. A local who we were unable to identify until years later, had been threatening our lives and the life of my grandfather by offering to set his house on fire with him in it. I started to have this vivid memory of the police coming to our home and hiding in the trees outside the house that night. It was then I realised, twenty plus years later, that feeling was still locked inside me. It had re-emerged spontaneously. Terror inside me had re-surfaced due to the woeful tale of what was happening to my two friends that I cared dearly about and had reignited that horror I'd clearly *never* let go of. It felt as if I was an eleven-year old child again, feeling helpless, shocked and in fear. The feeling of having your life threatened was back inside of me, as if it was yesterday, even though it was happening to somebody else. I somehow could still relate to it. The thing is, I didn't know what to do about what I had been told, and so I'd tried to block it out. It was a horrible situation to find myself in. But in that second, I somehow knew what I had to do.

I found my way to a police station quite some miles away from where I was staying. I had walked and hitchhiked with no money, no phone. In hindsight, it was a crazy move, but I just knew I had to get help to overcome this fear. Maybe by helping them I'd heal my child-self too who had been too young to help anyone, and given that I had (only a few days before) fully believed that I was never going to see another day, something inside me told me that I *had* to give a statement to the police, in case I did in fact, die. I knew that someone had to know about it and it made sense that I tell the police, as my friends were clearly not prepared to go themselves.

The expression on the police man's face was interesting, to say the least. I wasn't sure he would take me seriously. But I bravely gave my statement to him anyway, and I then phoned my friends from the police station to let them know I had given a statement on their behalf. I felt like I had nothing to lose since facing and accepting the idea of my own mortality. I know it seems that I was being irrational and was probably experiencing a high state of anxiety at that stage of my life but still, I felt it was something that had come into my awareness for a reason and as always, I followed the 'voice'. Luckily, after the whole ordeal, a very friendly, kind police man drove me back to where I was staying. In the car he said, "It sounds as if you've been over-working and could do with a nice rest". I realised I must have been gone for hours but whatever I had done in that time, felt like it had significance. Once I had gotten that off my chest, I felt lighter, but I also knew I needed help in case the terror manifested again, and I couldn't cope. Everyone needs a little help sometimes, so I decided I would speak to my G.P. and ask for a consultation with my local Mental Health team.

Four things I knew:

- It was time to ask for help
- I refused to let my fears take over again
- Perhaps they could help
- Action in the direction of your inner wisdom is all that matters to create new results

Luckily, Dr Hamilton had known me since childhood; she knew about my head injury at university playing hockey and so I requested a brain scan at the hospital, which was granted to me. I knew I needed to know what was going on inside my head and to eliminate any neurological issues. Mostly, because I had asked for help, I was sure I wanted to get better; that made a *huge* difference. I felt like I was on the road coming home to myself now. I went to see a psychiatrist in the NHS Mental Health team recommended by my G.P., and I was so fortunate for what played out next. Two amazing mental health nurses (who had already been to see me, for my "crisis" at my parents' house where I was staying) had now informed me that I would be *offered* anti-depressants on my initial consultation with the psychiatrist: thank goodness for the forewarning. Although I was much more settled by now, I was still feeling very vulnerable and without being pre-warned about the medication, I'm not sure if I would have taken it or not. Instead, I listened to what the psychiatrist asked me and challenged him on his questions. I told him that if I asked my past coaching clients the questions he was using to 'define' how I was feeling, they would be depressed too! He had -in no way- even *explored* the root of what was going on for me, it was all symptomatic and generalised.

In my mind, he had *not* asked me the right questions that would give him an idea of the root problem, and so could never find a solution and luckily, I knew that medication was not the path. Like I said in previous subchapters, the *quality* of the questions defines the experience. Well, my experience with the psychiatrist was not the answer I was looking for.

Before my psychological *malaise*, I had been professionally trained, certified, and practised Neurolinguistics in my coaching business. I knew I was not depressed in the 'medical' sense of the word. I had just not been honouring my truth, facing my deepest fears and asking the right questions. I asked the psychiatrist how anti-depressants would change how my husband and I communicate with each other. He said, "fair enough" but not before attempting to instil fear, "...well, you're only likely to have another relapse if you don't take them".

Again, my inner voice spoke. I knew that I was right and didn't need them. I didn't give in and he let me go. I pledged that one day, I would walk back in there and teach the Mental Health team some of what I knew, in case other people who were less informed about how the mind works, were also placed on anti-depressants with side effects and health warnings such as, "This can shorten your life". There was no way that the voice inside me would be drowned out by medical 'blockers' of my intuition. Fortunately, I was buddied up with Emma, an 'early intervention' member of the Mental Health team. We were on the same level, she was into mindfulness and Yoga and so she understood where I was coming from. I was also graced with Emma's support six weeks earlier than normal and so I levelled myself out really quickly. Why? *Because I had bravely asked for help.*

'Ask and you shall receive', the bible says, and that's exactly what happened. I had avoided the medication route and believe me, in my case this is rare. Six weeks later, I was told by a mental health nurse on one of her home visits that I was only one of two people in the whole county she was visiting, that was *not* taking anti-depressants. She also asked me how I had managed to balance myself out so quickly without them, having never witnessed any such recovery in her experience. I told her that self-coaching with Neuro Linguistics processes, yoga, meditation, playing the piano, writing and drawing, walking in nature, the love and support of my parents, some key friends (Karen, my Yoga teacher), kinesiology (with Lise and Gitti) and of course, talking to Emma in the Mental

Health team got me back to health. I had an absolute determination to get better because with support, I knew I could.

Don't get me wrong, I knew that certain other people were perhaps looking at me like I was a nutter. I wasn't surprised: I felt like a nutter, but I didn't focus on those people. I only focused on people who *believed* in me and understood that I was going to get better. I knew I was going to be okay if I didn't hide my mental breakdown and kept accepting positive help. Meanwhile, the brain scan came back - all clear. With no physical damage, I knew I could work through the rest of it, one step at a time and get myself back on track. My advice to anyone struggling with mental illness is to seek help but *only* from those who do not want to simply medicate you and send you off with a quick fix. Ask for help from your deepest voice *first* that will lead you to your 'highest good' and lead you to people who will be helpful at just the right time. Now it sounds much too easy to suggest you can just do that by lying at home visualising being rescued, and it will just happen. Here is the irony, I did spend time lying at home, waiting for someone to come and rescue me! That was my first step. The difference is, after I visualised it, I then received inner guidance on where to go and what to do!

So, you must do this: first, accept that you aren't feeling good and have a beautiful desire to work towards feeling better, it really is that simple. Then visualise your rescue or the people you would like to help you. Even the intention itself will begin to set you free. Then you will get what I call a 'nudge' to action, or a sign to speak to someone- do it. That's how it works.

Chapter 2 - What Do You Want?

2.1 - Identify What Makes You Happy

In the last chapter we talked about setting the intention to get better, combined with a little support. Of course, this question needs to be asked:

"What do I *want* to happen?"

You see, it is easy to be general and say that you want things to improve, but how can you know what that improvement would be if you don't know what you truly *want*.

Often, we are so accustomed to doing things habitually, that we spend our lives just accepting what we have created up until now. You may have heard of a rather clever man who knew a thing or two about this idea. His name was Einstein, and he famously said:

"Insanity means doing the same things over and over again and expecting a different result."

Well the thing is, when you are not consciously aware of what you want to manifest, you just run all your old programs in a loop and do the same thing repeatedly, even though the results don't change. This is the purpose of the pain we experience, it is telling us that something must *change* and yet because we are creatures of habit, we don't want to.

So, let me ask you now, "What do you want?" It sounds so simple, and on the surface, it *is* a simple question. Earlier when we were talking about quality questions, we talked about asking productive questions to get better and clearer answers, and now if you dwell on the question itself, you will find that there is more than one way to ask the same thing. For example: ask yourself, "What *do* I want?" If you don't receive an intuitive answer when you sit with it, try asking it with emphasis on a different word: "What do *I* want?" Even add some words in for clarity: "What do I *really* want?". This helps open up the question creatively in order to get the answer you seek.

My clients sometimes feel like running away at this point. Why is this question so *hard* to answer? Because when you face that question and have the courage to answer it authentically, it can create waves of feelings that are so unbearably uncomfortable that you might want to run a mile. It might involve changing cities, leaving a spouse, taking some time alone, changing career, leaving something comfortable; your truth sets you free, but it also causes unrest to that part of yourself that was under the illusion you were doing just fine as you were. Like we mentioned before, when you face yourself and ask for what you want, you can find yourself in a space that is far away from where you are sitting right now, in your current reality of life. Sometimes, it can be an apparently selfish decision because you have perhaps-up until now-been living for other people and doing what they expect of you. Doing what you *really* want (what your soul yearns for) usually means that there are changes that need to take place and that might involve other people.

This involves a scary level of self-responsibility because the only person who can make those changes are YOU, and what a thought that is.

What usually follows is the self-doubt that you can't make those things happen. You ask, "Can I really have that?" Suddenly on cue, the tiny voice creeps in, the one that worries and doubts your abilities. If you've never experienced this negative inner voice, then you are one of the only people that I know of (to date) that has not experienced it, and I can presume you may be lying to yourself. After all, it's not a voice that we care to freely admit we have. The good news is we are all on the same boat; I strongly believe that we as human beings are *all* inflicted with this little critical voice inside our minds, it helps us to believe that we are not deserving and keeps us from action. It also reminds us that in order to succeed, there surely has to be some suffering attached and so we stay stuck where we are. There is honestly no easy way to switch this voice off, but there is one way to jump straight into the proof that you can have it and do it:

Decide.

You can think about doing something all you want, I did for years and I knew what I was thinking was right, but it was only when I took a new action towards my dream life that it actually happened in reality. There is no magic formula for doing what you know is right for you, the magic only exists in your feelings that tell you it is possible. So, how do you just decide on something so new and frightening? I like this definition:

"A decision is cutting off from any other possibility".

You have to make it specific and follow through. I know that the bigger the decision, the bigger the doubt, and that is why some people reach a certain level of success and just stop or self-sabotage. Some of us have trained our minds to overcome that initial voice of doubt on the small things, so it doesn't always stop us in our tracks at the first hurdle. However, when the dream gets bigger, so does the fear of it. What would life be like for you if you could just switch off that voice in your head? The one that stops you from doing the things that make you feel extraordinary? I guarantee that at some stage, even now, doubt has held you back; imagine what might happen if you *decided* that even if you feel doubt, you'll do what you need to anyway? After all, if you feel *good* thinking about what you want, then that is your gut telling you it is right, and why would that happen if it wasn't? But when the seed of doubt is planted by our mind or somebody else, it is like a weed in our garden of happiness. It takes root and then we can easily- if not aware that we are doing it- *nurture* it until it becomes an entire tangled garden of fear and misery. If we don't weed out those doubts and send them packing, guess what happens? Not only do the roots get deeper but its buddies come to join the party, because the doors have been opened for more and more negative thoughts to attach to it and snowball into anxiety or even depression.

If you are cultivating and nurturing doubt, then you will live and see your whole life that way, it is really that simple.

Below are a few steps to get you from a loop of doubt and fear and back into focus on what you actually want:

1. **Take some time to simply identify what actually generates feelings of happiness inside you**: This will help you to evaluate where you are in your life right now and focus you on the present. When you identify what happiness means to you, it is your first step to setting a purpose. Let's face it, did any of us really land on this planet with the *purpose* of being scared and miserable? Remind yourself of this. If we never stop and take the time to recall that our goal is to be as happy as possible, it is just too easy to fall in to the trap of settling for less. And why would *anyone* want to do that to themselves?
2. **Have some courage.** I believe that it can take great courage to choose a life fully aligned with the things that make you feel happy, but I'll share a meaning of courage, which I was taught years ago:

Courage is Doubt + Commitment + Action

So, don't think that courage means you are not allowed to have doubts, you still can. Just don't dedicate your entire focus to those doubts, have a more empowered focus. Tell yourself that it is scary, you *do* have doubts but that you know deep inside, they are temporary so long as you have the *commitment* and take the *action* to prove it.

Here's three examples of decisions I made that were tough for me because I was filled with doubt:

- Quitting Smoking
- Leaving my Marriage
- Moving to Cyprus to write this book, even though my twelve-year-old daughter did not want to come with me and didn't.

There were plenty more but with each of these decisions, I had to deeply face myself, find my courage to overcome every notion of doubt and move forward in a direction more aligned with what made *me* feel happy. That is not easy to do.

Smoking is a habit, an addiction. In some ways, so is an unhappy marriage. Even staying in one country and not following what you know you should do is living out a comfortable habit. In all three examples, I had to *shift* either habit, home, or place, and it was an upheaval every time. However, the new actions led to new opportunities and so I had broken out of old results and into better, more magical possibilities.

2.2 - How Do You Know What Makes You Feel Happy?

In order to help you understand what makes you happy, and how I found my passion again, let me continue with my story to illustrate some of the ups and downs that occurred in the six years after I left my husband and home. Like I said before- doubts, pain and fear can all still exist when you make a firm decision to leave your comfort zone, but if you think that you haven't made the right decision just because the after-effects feel initially 'bad', then I'm going to continue to show you the light at the end of the tunnel.

For example, one day, I was lying on my sheep skin rug in my meditation room. My journal was in front of me, my pen was in my hand and a flood of colouring pencils were strewn on the floor beside me. It was a Sunday morning. I'd just finished my yoga, Pilates and meditation practise; something that I had done before breakfast for years. The beautiful morning sunlight was shining down through the roof window onto my journal and there I was again, back in my peace (just like that); something I hadn't been feeling for a very long time. This was just after my divorce, which was the final result of my decision to leave- I'm proud to say I had saw it through to the end. I am not going to lie and pretend that the divorce freed me fully then and there, in fact, it was still an excruciating journey. At this stage, I was a full-time mother and had been for six years. I admit that's how long it took from separation to divorce and it was like a slow painful death.

As you can imagine, whatever friendship or connection my husband and I had (before I told him I wanted to leave) was now in tatters; it took a nervous breakdown, two years of failed mediation and one court case before it was finally resolved, albeit on paper. I realised that when someone is hurt by your actions, they probably don't exactly want to make your life easy, and so the trust between me and most of his side of the family broke down. I've heard it's what you should expect in divorce situations, and while I feel it could have been more amicable, I definitely learnt what I needed to from it and moved on. Like I said, however, it took a *while* to get there.

Healing is progressive and with every challenge you overcome, you get just that little bit brighter, so long as you are always moving forward on 'gut' decisions. At the end of my divorce, I had invested so much energy into the situation that it seemed impossible to turn any of it into something positive, and I was exhausted beyond the point of exhaustion. I had been working so hard at caring for our daughter whilst doing everything I could to regain my health. I had become aware that my body was showing signs of fatigue in many ways. Firstly, I had adrenal fatigue – a fight or flight response of my body. My digestive system had not been working properly, which showed up as food intolerances (maybe my fearful mind was fighting my 'gut' feelings). To add insult to injury, a minor cancer scare cropped up on my left breast; a reflection of my need to be nurtured. I knew from my profession as a Neurolinguistics practitioner, and a decade of experience in a number of healing modalities, that there is a powerful connection between your thoughts, the emotions (that are generated by your thoughts) and the results that show up in your life – including in your physical body. I have discovered time after time, the connection between thought forms and the manifestation of physical symptoms; I witnessed it in my own body and in also in those of my clients. For further understanding of this, Louise Hay's book, *You Can Heal Your Life* explains the quantum physics of this phenomenon beautifully.

I knew I had to decide again to keep going, keep searching and finding better ways of thinking, being and acting out health on all levels. I booked myself in to the King Fisher Centre in Glastonbury to detox and re-boot my physical system, which I knew would help kick-start my mental and emotional well-being; I wanted to get back into peak physical shape too! More positive decisions ensued: one week of juice fasting, three colonic irrigations, inversion tables and body work. Not to be gross, but the experience of witnessing 30+ years of undigested matter from my colon disappear down the plug hole was an awakening experience in itself, it showed me how toxic I had been, before I decided to clean it up. Afterwards, I felt like I became more physically connected with another part of my body that I hadn't really taken much notice of before; I was facing yet another part of myself.

When I came home from my retreat, I had an "automatic switch off moment". It was brilliant. Every time I made a good decision, my body and mind rewarded me, then I was onto the next challenge of healing, but things were definitely improving and shifting.

Suddenly, I became aware of the foods that made my body weak; I seemed to know exactly what they were and have no desire for them. This is the gift of consciously deciding and becoming aware. This occurred in exactly the same way as when I stopped smoking 10 years earlier, when I just "got it" and had no desire to smoke again. Just like that. All because I had decided to do something good for *me.* I was on a mission to get healthy: I worked with nutritionist, Amy Desborough and Kinesiologist Lise Matthews to identify specifically what nutrition I needed to re-build not just my digestive system but also, all other systems that were struggling – this included my adrenals and brain. I seem to remember that depression and anxiety were in the mix too and dealing with the physical side of things truly helped.

Every few months, I was muscle tested to see what my body needed in the form of nutrients and I started to have really big breakthroughs in my health because I *made* it important. My energy started to return, along with clarity of thought and my motivation to "get back out there".

My coaching business had been on hold for six years, as I had not been in any space to hold a positive vision for others but somehow, I knew that my love for helping people to find their brilliance was brewing again. Whilst re-building my health, I was gaining the energy to return to doing what I loved. You see I *love* coaching. I love helping others to shine. It's one of the things that makes me feel really happy. That's how I found out what my passion was, by deciding to fix myself first and then suddenly, it became clear that the love I was giving myself was spilling out into the world and was re-igniting my love for helping others. For me, my 'happy place' is facilitating shifts in the consciousness of others, so that they too start to become unstuck from hidden beliefs and energetic blocks that have been holding them back for years. Sometimes, great realisation happens to them in a matter of minutes, and to witness it is extraordinary and humbling.

I'm thinking now of Jay here. At the time of writing this book in May 2018, Jay helped me to cross Birmingham airport in a wheelchair, as I had snapped two ligaments in my ankle and could not walk unaided. By the time he'd taken me to check in (five minutes later), we'd established the root cause of his stutter from years earlier in a casual conversation. When I passed through Birmingham airport eight weeks later, I was overjoyed to hear how he had "heard" what I had said and adopted the simple new strategy that I had suggested. Jay had excitedly recalled that his stutter had reduced by 60% and he now felt confident to work at his customer desk again. To date, whenever I pass through Birmingham airport, Jay heads straight over to let me know how he's doing. My heart overflows with joy. *This* is what happiness feels like to me. It totally lights me up to see the shifts that can take place in someone and quickly.

Similarly, I had met Niamh Kromo (on Facebook of all places) back in October 2016. Niamh was a very inspirational mindset coach, who lived in Switzerland. She'd asked me the question:

"What does happiness mean to you?"

This became the title that looked back at me from my journal on that Sunday morning. That is why I was in the zone; I spent about two hours drawing what made me feel happy. It was so simple yet effective. I had identified:

- The things that I had done in my life (past)
- The things that I was currently doing (present)
- The things that I would like to do, that I believed would create feelings of happiness (future)

I allowed my imagination to take over. I did not limit myself. For me it was simple things. For you, it might be something more complex but either way, the focus on it is how the answers come. That Sunday morning, as I drew and drew my 'happy' things, I could feel every cell in my body lighting up at the thought of embracing these things – past, present and future. I felt excited at the thought of what I had drawn. I was looking at the next chapters of my life.

2.3 - What is it 'Not'?

Sounds like a simple question: *What doesn't make you happy?*

I believe that if you identify what you didn't enjoy or what doesn't feel good, it can help you to move away from those things. You don't have to dwell on them because of course, that creates a snowball of misery, but at least be aware of patterns you don't like, so that you do not repeat them. For example, I remember my first job. I bet you do too. I was sitting next to my mate Rob by the river at lunch time in 1998, not long after finishing University. I was so bored. It was my first proper fully paid "grown up" work experience (the majority of my work experiences up until then had been from about the age of four on our family farm and holiday cottages). Rob had wisely told me, that "you've got to have your bad chips to appreciate your good chips". He was indeed right. I felt so unfulfilled and uninspired back then as a recruitment consultant, but that feeling of discomfort is exactly how I kept moving forward. One week later, I was head hunted to another recruitment consultancy, for more pay and less hours. Why? Because Rob had already jumped ship from the company where we worked together, recommended me to his new employer and I was in. I wasn't sure what I wanted to do as a career, right from the word go, I just followed my inner voice.

Once upon a time, I thought I wanted to be a PT instructor, during my CCF (Combined Cadet Force) days at school. I was a pretty good athlete that had peaked too soon and injured my Achilles tendon after winning the English Schools 800m National Championships in London, aged 16. Unfortunately, when I could no longer run, guess what happened? Instead of seeing it as a new direction (being an athlete forever was clearly not my ultimate purpose), I began to smoke! Cigarettes crept in and with that, a downward spiral began in my physical abilities and my self-esteem. I began drinking too; nothing serious, just the usual experimentation with booze that can so easily go with the territory of being a teenager. You see, when you do what you love and continually make gradual progress, your confidence increases, but equally, when something goes wrong it can stop you in your tracks. Ironically, it was the race 'tracks' that had been taken from me. I knew back then that I had natural abilities that had now been taken away by injury. I had won school competitions both at county level and the nationals but all of a sudden, it was game over. My ankles had had enough, my Achilles tendons were over stretched and agonisingly painful, and I could hardly walk. This was not a happy time for me. I could not do the things that previously I could do *well*, and I couldn't win races any more.

At the time, I wasn't fully aware of the emotional impact of having to deal with suddenly not being able to perform at my best and living with pain, every day. Each ankle had been getting worse and I didn't know how to make it better.

It was only in later life, that I came to trust the notion that "everything happens for a reason" but back then, I had to struggle to come to terms with my new life. Turns out I'd been testing my emotional muscles for the 'new life' I would have to create for myself later (when I would leave my marriage).

Fortunately, at the time of my injuries, I had other options at school. I could play team sports. I wasn't the fastest any more with my ankle injury, but I had strategies of how to be a damn good team player, it seemed imprinted in me. I had a natural affinity for sports, it's in my family and luckily, it has been passed down to my daughter too. Of course, I did not feel happy at being side-lined from running and feeling unable to win races anymore. I didn't feel good that I could not compete and perform at my best or excel anymore on the hockey pitch. My fitness was low, my ankles hurt, but I could still play at least, so I made the best of it. It did not feel as fulfilling as before, but it *did* mean that I could develop being a 'team' player. Working with others for a common goal meant being a part of something that is more than "just about me"; something that would set me up for my life's work of serving others. Every 'bad' chip I was dealt allowed me to develop or look at another aspect of myself.

Even as a child, I had been brought up on a very busy farm in West Wales. I had learnt about hard work, team work and working for oneself from day one. I feel totally grateful for this grounded, wholesome start to my life, and I guess the injury just jump-started me back into that wholesome approach to life. However, it was well-balanced in the sense that I also knew how to be completely independent. At 11 years of age, I was sent to boarding school. In fact, it's where my athletics, sports and music interests took off. It's also where I learnt a lot of lessons about who I was and what did and *did not* make me feel happy. Although, I must say I was not consciously aware of this at the time, I just got on with it. It was in later life that I looked back and connected the dots; realising how important my early life was in helping to determine how I make decisions and thank God for it, or I may not have had the strength to be so bold in my actions.

I finished my A-levels at 18 and felt clear that there was nothing about the idea of university that felt right for me at that time; this might have been my very first adult decision to go against the grain. Because I wasn't feeling excited about the idea of going to university, I decided to head to Australia on my own for a year. Again, I just followed the feeling; it felt right but it didn't exactly sound logical or safe. I had never even flown before nor had I even had a "proper job" working for someone else. My holidays had been spent helping on the farm, going to the beach, helping with the holiday cottage business that my parents ran, and having fun with friends. However, in my boarding school, there were international GAP students; Australian students who had finished their equivalent of A Levels but no student from *our* school had gone over to Australia before. Nevertheless, I contacted St Katherine's School and put myself forward. I got the job. It entailed home and board for twelve months in a foreign country, in the safety of a school environment but it was still very daunting. I cashed in my life savings, booked my Quantas flight, got my visa and left the U.K. to embark on my first teaching experience away from the UK. I had no idea what I was letting myself in for, but I made the decision to follow a strong feeling; I had to do something *different*, to not follow the crowd for the sake of it but instead follow my instinct.

On the plane I had reflected: My athletics and sports career had been cut short through injuries, and I hadn't made the mark with my A-level results. My grandmother had died unexpectedly just before my exams and I had taken it rather badly. She was the first person that I felt close to that had died and I was experiencing grief for the first time. Isn't it funny that every time in my life to date that

I have decided to do something for *me*; something scary that feels like the right thing, (something that has been buried within me) comes up to be looked at and processed? It is almost like every time you live your truth; *the whole truth comes out*. This feels like pain, but it is wonderful, simply because you cannot heal yourself unless you become aware of what is hiding beneath the smiles.

When I returned from abroad a year later, I was 19 years of age. My brother in law then asked me the question, "What do you want to do when you are older, Rachel?"

The answer that came to me was:

"Whatever it is that allows me to *feel* happy".

What I had learnt and realised by the time I was 19, stuck. Because over twenty years later, the same holds true for me. The Dali Lama says that happiness is "doing the things you love with those that you love". I didn't need to know what I wanted to *do* and still don't in many ways, there are still endless possibilities. But I had realised early on that what was important to me was "being happy", and being around those who make me happy, so I followed that bliss as much as I could.

Sometimes surface happiness is not 'true' happiness; therefore, you must follow your gut on it. I know now that one of my roles in this lifetime is to help others learn how to overcome the restless mind and consistently create deep feelings of fulfilment and joy in their lives, naturally and ethically. Of course, in my opinion, fully understanding and appreciating happiness is to also to understand what it is *not*. When we experience the contrast of happiness, then we can fully appreciate what it feels like to be happy, and that is how happiness gets to feel so good. I strongly believe that anything that takes us away from a feeling of being authentically aligned with our own truth will fundamentally destroy our feelings of happiness in the end anyway.

There is much more to this. We have not even started yet. I will demonstrate what I mean, as you read on.

2.4 - How Does That Make You Feel?

"Everything that you do is to *feel* a certain way".

I love this statement and its' simplicity, so let's think about that for a moment. Our feelings are crucial, it is what it is all about. We all have free will to make choices, so we need to ask if the choices that we make in terms of what we 'choose' to think about and the actions we take (or don't take) are the cause of feelings of 'pleasure' or 'pain'?

According to one of my mentors, Christopher Howard, "We are the sum total of the choices that we make". So, if this is true, why wouldn't we want to consistently make *great* choices for ourselves that make us *feel great*? Some choices that we make however, can create pleasure in the moment and then create pain in the long term. I know this one all too well. Remember when I chose to smoke? That was a 13-year habit of choosing to fill myself up with something that was toxic and life threatening to myself and others. Any rational, intelligent person simply wouldn't entertain the idea of smoking, would they? There are a lot of clever people in the world who have fallen in to this trap, knowing it is bad for them, but do nothing to change it, because the short-term relief is enough for them. The consequences are dangerous, however. I never thought about it much at the time, especially when I was younger, it was just "something that I did". I wasn't really thinking about the long-term. Instead I was gradually undermining my physical, mental and emotional well-being without me even being consciously aware of it. How true is this for other choices that we make in our lives?

We have 70,000 thoughts running between our subconscious and conscious minds every day.

So, ask yourself these four questions:

- How many of them are positive?
- How many judgements do we make in a day?
- How many actual decisions do we make in a day?
- How many of those thoughts, judgements, decisions and actions that we take every day create a feeling of happiness inside of us? And I mean, REAL happiness?

One of my clients who I helped to break a 20+ year smoking habit (in about an hour) a few months ago, texted me to say that he had recently been thinking about smoking again, amidst a challenging life situation. Fortunately, he made the decision to work *through* things without the crutch of the cigarette. This is all it takes, a firm decision and no looking back. At times of crisis when we are feeling most challenged, it is so easy to revert to the things that we feel give us a "crutch".

Unfortunately, some of those things just don't do us any long-term favours, do they?

I had smoked and struggled with quitting for years, feeling a bit like a schizophrenic in terms of feeling constantly split between the ideas of "I want one, no I don't, yes I do, no I don't", and then looping in a cycle of self-punishment after giving in and having one (and feeling rubbish with myself afterwards). I finally quit when I understood that the cigarette changes *nothing*. There is nothing positive that a cigarette can give to anyone that they cannot give to themselves. I have since spoken to many smokers who wish to stop their habit. They often give the following reasons for their addiction:

- Helps me relax
- Gives me breathing space, a stop gap from work
- Gives me something to do when I get bored
- It gives me something to do with my hands
- It's a social thing, my friends do it
- I like to have one with a drink – the two go hand in hand
- Rebel status – "No one's going to tell me what to do"
- Peer pressure

My belief is that the cigarette simply represents all the s**t about yourself that you have not resolved yet. The smoker attaches themselves to a thing that they think will help them in some way, but in fact, it does quite the opposite and they can't let go of it, which, then leads them in to an ever-decreasing spiral of s**t. So, if you smoke, what are you not letting go of?

When we truly value our life to the extent that we want to nurture ourselves by making great decisions that are life enhancing each and every day, and when we commit to being fully aligned with what makes us feel truly happy, how can there be *any* space for thinking bad thoughts about ourselves or other people, or having bad habits that lead to our degeneration? I strongly believe that many of us have forgotten how to love ourselves wholeheartedly and that is the only reason we need to fill ourselves up with distractions.

Our thoughts can be equal killers if the mind is not navigated masterfully. You will think everything is 'OK', then you won't see it coming, just like the cancer on my breast that the doctor found after my divorce. It was minor, thankfully, but I knew it was a warning. I knew I'd been feeling beyond stressed during the ongoing divorce process, but I was taking such good care of myself on so many other levels, that I was surprised and a bit frightened to say the least. I asked the doctor how long I had before further investigations were to take place and he told me, 'six weeks'.

"Great" I said, "I'll resolve it in four".

I knew I had created the problem and I had to become aware of it and get to work.

Four weeks later, I discovered that it had cleared itself up after constant morning meditations where:

- I was given insight into what was going on
- I discovered the belief system that had generated the cancerous growth
- I received an answer on how to resolve it

No one cured me, I just listened deeply to myself and it healed all on its own. Four weeks later, I was tested with kinesiology and it was confirmed that the cancer was no longer showing up as a threat in my body. Two weeks after that, the NHS doctor confirmed the same.

If we all start giving ourselves full attention and love every day, then magic and miracles can happen. I just began noticing when I was:

- Eating the wrong foods or quantity of foods for optimum health
- Getting up and going to a job every day that did not feel fulfilling
- Attracting or remaining in a relationship that did not serve me

These are just a few of the things that I had to experience and then let go of, to understand the importance of always listening to my feelings. It has been said that love is the most powerful healing force in the universe. So, when we remember how to:

- access the wisdom of our hearts
- take daily steps to ensure that we think and act in a way that releases fear
- take daily steps to ensure that we think and act in a way that fills us with feelings of love

Then we are well and truly on the path to 'real' happiness.

So, ask yourself now - *How do your daily thoughts and actions make you feel?*

Chapter 3 - How Do You Want to Feel Every Day?

3.1 - Anything Less Than Happy Isn't Really Worth It

I know how I want to feel every day. I am also not naïve to the fact that the universe will throw things at you, to see how *committed* you are to receive what it is that you *say* you want. Without obstacles, you'll never know what your *truth* is. You cannot know what makes you happy until you really experience what doesn't and eliminate it. By staying true to my heart and just working through all the things that came up (that didn't feel so good), I was able to transcend the circumstances every time. Does that mean that as I progressed, I had no challenges? Of course not. The difference is, I also knew deep down they were helping me grow, I didn't fight against them, I worked *through* them. As you know, I had many opportunities for growth during my breakup and divorce.

When I decided to leave, I was essentially ostracised and undermined in my role as a mother. I wasn't sure what to *do* to fix it, (I never know until I just tune in and listen to what must happen next).

One thing that kept coming up was a lesson I had learned in Don Miguel's book on Toltec wisdom, *The Four Agreements*, where he states, "Don't take anything personally". This was a big lesson for me. I had to *accept* that more than 50% of my daughter's family unit were officially unreachable; they had essentially ignored me and pushed me out. I had wanted to be free, and so they let me 'go' in the harshest sense of the word. Their hearts were closed. I worked through it and realised with compassion that I needed to let go of other people's opinions of what I had done and continue to follow my truth. It was not personal, and I *had* to let it be what it was. Don't get me wrong, I didn't *want* this outcome, I still wanted to be part of the family unit, at least at the level of being Amber's mother, and I wanted to be valued for that role, but the reality was: I wasn't going to get that outcome, it was out of my hands.

You cannot change other people, only yourself. Even the Dali Lama once said that "not getting what you want can be an incredible stroke of luck", so after five years of feeling ostracised from my husband's family, I realised that it was a blessing because it taught me something. Everyone is on their *own* journey, with their own level of consciousness and I can't change that, but I can have the wisdom to be 'OK' with it. I decided to let go of anything that fed the drama. I stopped attempting to build relationships with others who "don't want to know" and focused my attention back on myself, where I belonged, because that was where my power was. This was huge for me because I knew the obvious gap between the in-laws and I, would be taking its toll on Amber, and it is hard for any mother to not consider how your child could be affected from adults 'not getting along'. Over time, I was able to free my mind of the fear that rose up inside me when Amber returned from family visits with them. It was a real blow hearing her say all the strange things that I believed were probably reiterated from them, because they couldn't have just come from her. I understand how a child works on a mental and emotional level (having helped hundreds of people, both adults and children to release trauma from their subconscious minds) and so I knew that unless this situation was resolved, it would be hard for everyone to let go of the past.

So, I did something different; instead of trying to 'fix' Amber's pain, I just kept myself right. I promised myself I would *be* the example of someone who could let go, rather than instructing her to do it, and not living it myself. It might not have seemed that way at the time, but I knew that this was *real* parenting at a source level; when she was the right age, she would come to realise that what I had done was *true love*. I know now that you cannot reach happiness until emotional destabilization is resolved through reaching a higher perspective; this is when balance can be restored. Everything else is "make believe" and only makes your mind feel good short-term, but as the saying goes, "The truth always comes out in the end".

Do you remember I said earlier that my friend Rob had told me "you've got to have your bad chips to experience your good chips', well, I thought back to that during this time and said to myself : Why invest any energy in focusing on positive relationships with people who "don't want to know"? Instead, I had better questions:

- How could I turn this in to something positive?

- What was it that I needed to learn?
- What was the blessing in it?

I had to trust that there was a higher purpose for things not turning out the way I wanted. I had exhausted myself getting to that point of realisation and when I had invested energy into what was *wrong* in the past, I just had more 'bad' things happen. I knew I had been facing fear after fear, but I trusted the whispers of my heart. Every time I did, I elevated myself back to the higher perspective of my purpose and my happiness levels rose. Anything less than feeling deeply happy and fulfilled isn't worth it in my opinion, but you have to first realise what superficial happiness is, and the underlying truth of real happiness that lives within. Luckily, my challenges helped me know what *didn't* feel good and that pushed me within myself.

So, if it is true that the universe provides exactly what we need in order to help us decide how committed we are to our purpose in life, I have *everything* to thank my failed marriage for. When it fell apart on the outside, I had no choice but to go inside. Outside was full of fear, drama and war, but where true happiness resides, those things can't get in. That is how I came to realise that it doesn't matter what goes on, 'out there'; as long as I feel deeply fulfilled, I know that I am on the path to joy.

A path to joy consists of being awake and in alignment with yourself. But how do you know that you are fully "awake" if you don't know that you are "asleep" in the first place? I can tell a mile away when someone's heart is closed, because mine was too, at one point. I had closed it down to protect myself from being hurt, and it was not a conscious choice. I remember when I realised this and had one of my first total awakenings. I was at my friend's house where I'd been invited to join in to a "Living in the Heart" ten-week process. This too was during my separation, when I felt that I had been punishing myself for too long. In this process, a number of us would meet every week and share what was happening for us. No-one would comment, we would simply witness; observe each other with no judgement and just be present. We were bound by confidentiality and no-one was to share who attended, nor the content of our discussions. It was a very simple, yet profoundly powerful process. We had created a space of allowance, where we could simply speak our deepest truths, fears and thoughts safely and it was humbling to just let it all flow.

For me, one of the realisations that occurred was that I was able to track back to the specific points in my life where my heart had closed to protect myself, and being 'awake' to those moments, freed them from my body. I was bullied as a child because I had been 'smart', and the other kids just took that to mean 'nerd', so I was able to begin letting that go, by realising I hadn't done anything wrong by being myself. I had also experienced some sexual abuse and I knew that had contributed to me closing down to others, because I was afraid that they would take advantage of me. As a Neuro Linguistics Re-Patterning Coach, I knew what I had to do with these realisations. I sought help from a friend, Sarah Middleton who was a *Journey* Practitioner and another fellow Reiki Master, to resolve these times in my life, now that I was aware of their effect. I believed that until I gained full resolution of what had happened in my childhood, I would continue to attract similar situations in my life. For instance, I remembered learning on my leadership training programme with Christopher Howard that we are holographic. What I mean by this, is that we attract in the "mate" who is at our equivalent level of consciousness, at that time. If we want to rise above it, we must be willing to not just let go of that level of awareness, but also the people connected to it. Most people (instead of doing this) beat the crap out of the *other* person (or people) involved, for what they reflect back in ourselves. The truth is that we have not resolved those negative qualities in ourselves and so we turn to blame.

Maybe at a deep level, my husband had done nothing wrong, I had just simply resolved a lot of things about myself and was ready to move on, because the relationship no longer supported the next phase of my journey. We were clearly in different spaces, and I was wide awake to it. I had to humbly allow our marriage to dissolve, from a place of love. I was doing my best to stay in this space, in the face of huge resistance from all fronts, often not managing it. I was frustrated at times, even angry but I realised that these emotions would pass if I didn't let them live there permanently. I knew I had the ability to heal no matter what and be stronger than ever before. I also trusted that whatever had happened to me had happened for a reason. I also knew that I would learn why, when I was ready.

If you remember, in 2010, I went to see my doctor (the one that I was warned would prescribe me medication) and as I sat reading a leaflet in the waiting room, I came across a paragraph that allowed me to know I was in the wrong place for healing. The leaflet stated that anyone who spoke to angels or felt that they were on a 'mission' were clearly suffering from symptoms related to being "bi-polar". Not for one second did I disempower myself and buy into this, because I knew without a shadow of a doubt that I had been connecting with angels for quite some time, and their guidance was nothing but pure love. I also *knew* that I had a mission in my lifetime and I was not going to let that pure feeling go because someone 'external' didn't feel the power of it. I had already received absolute clarity on what I wanted to do on this planet during one of my leadership programme modules, *Design your Destiny*. I knew I wanted to show people how to tap into their own truths and become free inside but of course, after reading that pamphlet, I decided to stay quiet and keep my connection with angels and my mission under the radar, until I was well and truly feeling totally balanced again and back on track with my work.

I made a pledge to myself that day, that I would come back and teach a way back to health without anti-depressants (which I can now say, I have). I decided from my experience, that there was a necessity for mental health teams to catch up on what was possible, in terms of how to overcome mental health challenges, naturally and safely. I was not seeking to replace what they had learned, merely add to it; show that there were other ways, but you must be 'awake' to them. When we don't have clarity on what makes us feel happy, we can walk around in a trance of disempowerment for years, making decisions that are not in alignment with our truth and blaming others for our own sense of lack, that is when we seek to medicate ourselves.

However, I must tell you that the heart never lies. Having the courage to face everything about yourself that does not feel right will empower you more than anyone or anything else.

What's worse than being asleep and disempowered?

In my mind, it's being awake and not *doing* anything about it, because you haven't got the tools, resources and support. That feels totally disempowering. However, I promise you that you have everything you need to begin, and it starts from inside. You just have to decide that you want the best for yourself. I decided long ago that I would never allow myself to be treated badly and instead create a life that would facilitate my freedom, and I chose to only surround myself with conscious, loving people in all areas of my life. I ensured that I blamed no one and didn't allow their blame to affect me either. Don Miguel once said,

"Nothing others do is because of you. What others say and do is a projection of their own reality, their own dream. When you are immune to the opinions and actions of others, you won't be the victim of needless suffering".

When I truly got this, I suddenly didn't care about being cut off from the family. I simply chose to perceive it as fantastic opportunity for growth. I realised how crazy I had been for buying into a lower level of consciousness that could have knocked me off my path, instead of really listening to what I wanted. When you don't listen to yourself, you are dangerously wide open to all the opinions of others.

For example, when I went into crisis in 2010, the words "bi-polar" came hurling down the phone towards me from my ex-mother in law. I knew she had no qualifications or expertise in this field and thankfully, I trusted myself or else I might have believed her. I didn't believe it in the doctor's waiting room, so I wasn't about it believe it then either. Imagine the impact that such an untruth would have on my daughter, if she and an entire family unit were to buy in to this "opinion" and keep it going. I wanted to teach Amber that living your truth is the only path to freedom and when you buy into labels created for you, that is what you will *become*; just another statistic, another person with a problem that needs symptomatic relief.

Of course, I knew the only way to be free was to let go of opinions. They couldn't know what was happening to me, because they were not me. I forgave them for not knowing me the way they thought they did, and I used an acronym in relation to them that helped me continue to let the pain go.

In this context, **FREE** stands for:

Forgiving **R**elatives **E**arnestly **E**nergises

This takes courage, commitment, dedication, soul-searching, focus and a lot of discipline. Most people do not want to let go of their story because blaming eases self-doubt, guilt, anger and sadness. It is necessary to detach yourself from those that appear to have hurt you; if you do, they no longer have any power over you and all the future empowerment you receive will be solely from you. No one can rob you of that.

3.3 - Live Life In The Moment Feeling Safe, Happy and Secure

Living life in a celebratory way (everyday, as if it was your last) was once quite a feat in my world, but I had to experience the level of suffering that I did for so long, to really appreciate the other side of it.

I live my life now by believing that there are no mistakes, only lessons to learn. I also believe that we get stuck in a loop and condemn ourselves to repeat the same mistakes if we do not choose to see the lesson and learn from it. It is all essentially *perspective* and so ask yourself the following, when you get discouraged:

- What perspective have I bought in to now, that is discouraging me?
- If I am tapping into doubt, is it mine or someone else's?
- Where did it come from?
- What can I do about it?

Then trust your body, as I do, to tell you what is happening.

I know that a thought generates an emotion that turns into a behaviour. This reflects the results that show up in our lives. I also strongly believe that thoughts which generate emotions have a massive impact on health. How can they not? If we are feeling safe, happy and secure and living in the present, where is the space for fear or anxiety? When we are stuck in a state of "futurizing"; that is, thinking of what might happen (or indeed dwelling on the things in the past that have happened), it can be crippling. For example, I had no idea what would happen during my divorce case. The court would decide what happened to Amber and I had no power there, except to trust that it would all work out the way it was supposed to. I had to provide medical evidence to prove I was sane and that was daunting, but once my medical records were submitted, I was in the clear. They confirmed I was fine and more than capable of looking after my daughter and myself. Of course, I was never going to ignore the fact that I had to have responsibility for my emotional state, and I had to balance my needs with Amber's in the future, no matter what they said. I would forgive myself and my ex-husband for everything. I began to send him healing and light from a distance, trusting that on some level he could feel this, and acknowledging his pain in this process too. I had to trust that it would all work out for the best.

You see, I could have imagined the worst, but the scenarios that we create in our heads are often an illusion and may never happen, so why try and bring them into being? We don't really know what is going to happen tomorrow. We can only ever respond to an ever-changing set of circumstances. We cannot control outcomes until we control how we think; we can play any perceived 'scary' scenario over and over again in our minds and sometimes we can even create it for real because we have focused on it so much – hence the "self-fulfilling prophecy" –because when we fear something and bring it into our reality once, we have proved ourselves to be right. So, guess what happens then? If we don't let go of the thought of it, it is likely that we will create it again. We'll repeat the pattern until we learn a new strategy that proves us wrong and brings us alternative evidence to back it up. This is why breaking habits of a lifetime can be excruciatingly painful, if you do not know how to control your thinking.

Life is never static, you cannot stop whatever is coming because we are all in a continual state of change. Take our bodies for example: our cells are changing every day, we cut ourselves and we heal. We're amazing, really, and always in constant flux. Worrying about it is not going to stop it moving forward. Instead, daily meditation takes us back to the present moment. It stops us focusing so hard on the future and the past and brings us to the reality of where we are right *now*. Every day I build my strength from a place of deep surrender and awareness in meditation; I tell myself that there is more going on than I can necessarily see, and I just connect with my heart. Every time I connect with my heart and stay in that feeling of deep reverence, nothing can touch me.

At the time of those court proceedings, my father said, "you must not be afraid of going to court". He also said, "your calm is your strength" and he was right. Because of daily meditation and my practise of constantly checking in with myself, I get more immune to the judgments of others. I may slip every now and again if I feel pain from someone's perception, but then I go back into meditation, and re-align myself. If you choose to meditate every day in the same way, you too will become non-negotiable about putting your needs first (in a highly ethical way) and if you take the action your heart advises, there will be *zero* room for doubt, fear or anxiety in your life.

Every day, you will fill up your cup of joy and in doing so, you will then be in a position to meet the needs of others.

3.4 - Set Your Own Precedent – Everyday

This morning I woke up *really* late.

As you know, I love to get up at 5am and start my day with the routine that I have been doing for over a decade. But today, when I opened my eyes and looked at the clock. It was 10am. That's five hours of being behind schedule in my world.

I suddenly experienced that feeling of 'missing out', when suddenly a huge chunk of time has vanished, and for a moment, it made me feel out of sync. You see, getting up early makes you feel prepared; like you have lots of time to get things done. I had witnessed this early rising with my father, who has been a total inspiration to me all my life. As a farmer, he always got up at 5am, totally chilled and massively productive, with an enormous amount of energy to run his business and estate. I guess I have been subconsciously influenced by this. Even my mother, who is downstairs right now, as I write, is doing almost exactly what she was doing in the first seven years of my life: being an entirely committed wife, business partner and extraordinarily supportive, loving mother. We tend to model those around us and so I was lucky to be born into such a dedicated, loyal, and supportive family.

Each day when I wake up and do my daily practise of meditation, I remember what I value in my family and what they have taught me: focus, determination and consistency. Waking up at the same time every morning is my precedent for the day: I tune in, tap into my truth, gain insight into my next step and act on it. It never lets me down. This morning was no different because even though I woke up late, I was able to forgive myself for needing that extra rest and jump back onto the day's requirements, not letting it pull me off track. Life might not always work out as you expect, but sticking to a general plan and having that precedent is enough. So long as you set the plan, be willing to change if it changes and get back up there, you will always be on path.

If you want to be successful, you must find out what you value, model those you respect and set your own precedent – everyday. It may not happen exactly as you planned every single day, but if you trust yourself and stay strong, you'll always quickly get back up from whatever knocks you down.

Chapter 4 - Time For Change

4.1 - Making The Decision to Change

In this book, we have talked about the impact of my decision to change my life, leave my family home, remember what I value and follow through on the action. It was never going to be easy, but I knew from day one, I was following my *life path*. Can you remember a time when you felt absolutely certain about your path in life? A time when you felt happy because you were just being *you*: doing what you love, living in the moment, and taking life one day at a time?

Even if you have not felt fully aligned with your passion in recent times, as a child, there would have been moments where you were busy having fun. This is how life should still feel, but as we grow up, it seems that we can veer off the path of certainty and watch other people have all the 'luck'. A friend of mine, Eric, once told me that "Luck is when preparation meets opportunity". If this statement is true, then this is very exciting, because in my mind, it implies that we are master creators of our own lives and are all capable of creating magic. Every thought we have, creates an emotion. Every emotion creates a behaviour and set of results, and in between every thought and emotion, there is a judgement about whether it feels 'right' or 'wrong'. Any choice that we make today has implications and consequences for the future and every action has a reaction (as does every non-action.) We can look to other people for guidance, we can buy every course on earth that promises us riches, joy or better relationships, but I believe there is no one-size-fits-all formula for happiness and that is why, even if we have the best teachers, we can still not get anywhere, unless we are listening to the greatest teacher inside of us: our heart.

To a certain extent we all operate differently: we each have a different set of needs at any given time and are all in various states of awareness about what those needs really are. No one is ever going to fully understand who you are and what you need more than you, because you are operating from your own set of experiences and emotional states daily.

The fact that reality is mostly subjective means that the ability to communicate our dreams to others can be difficult, and not getting others to *share* in our vision, hinders any ability to "perform" at our highest potential, both now and in the future.

So, if you wish to live life on your terms, you must constantly listen to *yourself* before you listen to anyone else. By going inside and getting answers, it is likely that you will discover some clutter that needs to be removed. By finding out how you *really* feel, you will uncover new resourceful ways of thinking, speaking and behaving in order to create the world you wish to live in – *your* world. Once you feel certain about how you want to live your life and go into the world with that dream confidently, it won't matter what objection you face, or advice you get; you'll stick to your own terms, and the only thing you'll change won't be your mind, but your circumstances.

So, how do you know when it's time for change? For me, when I'm not on path, I feel some sort of mental, emotional or physical *pain.*

That's it, and it is always stemming from the same source:

Feeling Out of Alignment with Truth.

My experience of truth is that it feels like *love,* and that anything out of sync with love is always *fear.* According to my friend Derek, "Love is the antidote of fear", because the two cannot co-exist.

4.2 - My Life, My Terms.

I was lucky in a way because I was always encouraged to be myself and was supported by my parents to do what I love. Even today, they give me the utmost respect and space to continue to write my book. I know everyone might not have this backbone of support from family and friends, but I am so passionate about helping you realise (if you haven't already), that you can have and do whatever you want in your life. There is only one thing that is holding you back and it is not a lack of anything in the world outside, the problem is always your *mind.*

While attending *Billionaire Bootcamp* in Santorini (a beautiful Greek island) a few months ago, I was reminded that "magic happens when talent meets passion". It's the second time I have had the opportunity to study the mindsets and strategies of billionaires in the last decade and spend time with others who are driven to create legacies in their lifetimes. My first experience of this training was in 2008 and I was absorbing new information on how to create my own legacy. I had wanted to model those that had already *done* it. What was really exciting, was coming back *this* year, (over ten years later) and realising that I *had* done it. I knew I now had enough experience of tuning in and being around the right people, to begin sharing it with the masses. This wasn't luck. I knew that I was sitting in the place where preparation had now met opportunity. Here I was on a beautiful island with some of the 'elite' and it was all a direct result of the sum total of choices I had made. Every one of those choices had come from inside me and had manifested beautiful and magical life experiences. Luck had nothing to do with it; I had created my own luck by following my heart.

In May 2017, I received a strong intuition that I was to let others into my daily practise and teach how I access the wisdom of the heart, so I had created a meditation model called *Rise and Shine*. Do you remember when I told you about the time when I walked out of the NHS building, and promised that the next time I walked back in, it would be to positively change something? Well, at the bootcamp this year, I received feedback that the *Rise and Shine* model had "the capacity to revolutionise the mental health system globally". This came from my mentor (and later, a clinical psychologist) showing me I was right to follow the deepest desires of my heart. That day as we shared a delicious Indian lunch, there was a beautiful painting of the Indian deity Ganesh painted on the wall next to us and I knew it was a sign. In the Hindu tradition, Ganesh is the son of Lord Shiva and the Goddess Parvati. He is known as the remover of obstacles, and when I lived in India for five months in 2004, I noticed that there was a picture of Ganesh at the entrance of many of the homes that I visited. Since then, I have often become aware of Ganesh's energy in my daily meditations. At times when I have felt particularly challenged, I have intuitively connected with the energy of Ganesh and called upon him to help clear all obstacles from my mind and path, with ease and grace.

I recall an extraordinary experience on Christmas morning, in 2011, six weeks after I had left my marital home. I was meditating in front of a huge bronze Ganesh in my friend's house. The inner strength that I felt return to me on that morning was extraordinary. I cannot express in words the visualisations and the full extent of what I experienced. Words do not do the experience justice. I could sense the strength of Ganesh in every cell of my body and had a deep knowing that everything would be alright. It was Christmas day, a time to be with family, and also the birth of Christ (consciousness) so this was a really significant day to realise that I too, was being reborn into a higher awareness. I was now separate from my husband and Amber for the first time. I did not feel overly happy but because of this new energy I was tapping into, I did feel safe-wanting only to be with myself- and sitting in acceptance of what was.

After I left Santorini in 2018, I called a clinical consultant psychologist in the UK, while I was in Cyprus. She knew my work intimately and we were casually chatting about it, when she echoed the same words as my mentor; she too confirmed that she felt my learning model had the capacity to revolutionise the mental health system, globally. I had goose bumps, it was exactly what I needed to hear to confirm that the inner voice I had all these years, was now matching all the outer voices: I was surely in alignment.

Some of the things I have said in this book have been painful for me to re-visit and talk about, but I cannot advise anyone to be honest with themselves if I can't, and so the context is important. It shows that you too can do anything you want, if you just follow your own inner whisperings. I'll repeat this fact until the end of time if I have to because all the answers to living life on your own terms come from inside. If you really honour your own voice, it will eventually manifest as the life of your dreams.

4.3 - Staying Centred

Each and every time I receive guidance, in whatever form it manifests, I have learnt that if I ignore or *don't* follow it, things do not flow in the way that makes me feel good. I lose my feeling of deep centeredness. I know when I am in a state of flow and when I am not. When I meditate, which I have done religiously since 2004, I get better and better at becoming aware of my own needs. It is during these periods of deep silence and connection, that I also receive my greatest feelings of peace.

Sometimes, I receive insights about the future. I cannot see everything, only what I need to see in that moment, which is why it is vital to make it a daily practise.

Here are some of the things that I get clarity on when I tune in to myself:

- I receive great clarity about my next steps in life
- I am shown my greatest fears (in terms of what I need to overcome) in order to get to that next phase of my life
- I get a moment to forgive the fact that I don't always get it 'right'
- I receive guidance from my heart and also get to connect with my angelic guides, or ancestors that have passed before me

When I haven't perhaps listened fully to myself during these times, my *body* will bring it to my attention instead. I am sitting writing this with my leg up, nurturing two damaged ligaments in my ankle, which I know has happened in response to not paying attention to something. In this case, I wasn't resting enough, I had been 'running around' and so life made sure that I couldn't physically do that to myself anymore. I needed a break. At times, I get so excited about sharing and teaching my work, that I overstretch myself –

mentally, emotionally and physically – as I find ways to help others learn what I know. My ankle was simply reflecting that "over stretching" pattern that I had subconsciously picked up from my hard-working farming family, during my childhood. While the ankle kept me 'grounded', I worked on my book instead and said 'thank you' for the incident, because I trusted that it was what I needed. This trust is what will get you through life: I have learnt how to overcome and move through overwhelm so that I can experience greater heights of achievement and enrichment in all areas of my life, by having this same trust.

All is perfect just as it is, and everything is happening to you because it *has* to. It's that simple. You just have to listen if you want to know its purpose. Sitting and doing my daily meditative, self-enquiring, self-coaching practise is what allows the continued unfoldment of my path. Everything that I learn each day, ensures that I am always deepening my awareness. I have discovered that the more centred and grounded I am, the more clarity I have, and that is why meditation needs to become a priority in life. It gives you access to all the advice and help you'll ever need, and it doesn't cost anything! With practise, you may also start to distinguish between the voice of the ego and a higher level of consciousness that is communicating with you. It is the voice of the ego that makes decisions seem scary, because the higher voice only speaks in tones of love. If anything feels 'bad' or fearful, it is because it is not 'truth'.

In fact, I love these definitions of F.E.A.R:

- False Evidence Appearing Real
- False Expectation Appearing Real
- Face Everything And Rise
- Face Everything and Run with it

Which one would you choose to adopt as a guiding principle in your life?

Have you ever experienced a time in your life where you felt crippling fear that has stopped you from moving forward or listening to yourself?

I bet you have, because I have many times, although I always bring myself back and never let it shut me down completely. When fear exists, my experience is that things "close down" inside me and on the outside too.

Things like:

- Creativity
- Trust
- Laughter
- Joy
- Progress

When feelings of fear arise, I can't even think properly. That's because my system has been filled with cortisol and adrenalin and so I'm in *fight or flight*, instead of being in *freedom and flow.*

I have been told that the three biggest fears that exist for human beings are:

- The fear of flying
- Fear of public speaking
- Fear of dying

Fortunately, I have overcome all of these.

Luckily, I never had a fear of flying, although I must admit, I have had some "no way I am doing that" moments at theme parks – especially roller coasters. I eventually got on those rides though, because once the fear kicks in, we tend to stop, so I just kept pushing through it because I knew if I didn't, it would always be a problem. As for public speaking. I am not sure how long I had a fear of it, but I definitely disliked the idea of standing up in front of a room, under a spotlight and talking about something on my own. I remember avoiding debating society in school for this very reason. Even at university, I let my fellow course mate Lilly take the lead there because I found public speaking petrifying.

Then I realised, that if I did not change my strategy of avoiding public appearance, I would never get my messages out there to the masses and fulfil my life purpose.

You know, waking up to your potential and then doing something about it, (with absolute certainty that you can), is the only way to develop an area of yourself. At one point, I knew it was time to get over my fear of public speaking or I would not progress. I knew that if I asked myself 'why' I wanted to overcome it, that the 'how' would follow, and my 'why' question was – "Do you want to live your life purpose of sharing what you know with the world?" I did, and so I had to get comfortable with speaking up. I used to feel really uncentered when I spoke publicly, from sheer lack of practise, I'd been avoiding it for so long. But when I got clear on why I am here, I focused, I practised, and I got over it. I decided I would open myself up to every opportunity to speak that I could. I had thrown myself into the deep end and with repeated practise- as with everything- I was able to remain deeply centred in the face of change.

4.4 - Keeping The Faith

Faith is essential. As you recall, there have been so many times where logically, faith should *not* have been enough. I had a nervous breakdown, I left my home, my husband, I had little to no contact with my husband's side of the family, I was worried about Amber and how she was feeling and most of all, I had temporarily closed down my coaching business, meaning that at a very basic level: I had no home, no income stream (to get a home) and no foreseeable plan.

If you have ever found yourself at a time like this, then you will understand how hard it is to keep the faith. The one thing I did have was a level of clarity that it was time for change. In some ways, it was a blessing but also a curse, because I was in extremely uncomfortable new territory. I now have the privilege of helping both the persecuted parents and children who are involved in negative divorce processes, but I couldn't have seen that at the time. All I had back then was blind faith.

It was not pleasant that I experienced what I experienced, but at least I am now well equipped to help others dramatically reduce the needless suffering that they encounter. Back then, something inside me had been yearning to come out and it was only by honouring that need that I got to where I am today.

I couldn't see that I would get well, or how. I just *knew* I would get well. I couldn't imagine how I would get back on my feet financially, I just *felt* it. I kept my faith. This is your key ingredient during all challenges. When you have the courage to face anything that is out of balance in your life and make peace with it, great healing will happen. It always comes from within.

Chapter 5 - The Plan

5.1 - Waking Up

Some mornings during my divorce, I'd often wake up worrying about my daughter. For any mother, during emotional upheavals that include your child, it's hard not to think the worst sometimes. I'd replayed fights in my mind (things that were said between the 'grown-ups') and wondered about the effects of my leaving. I knew from studying Neurological Patterning, that children pick up on their parents' patterns of behaviour and play them out in their own lives, sometimes without even realising it. For example, Amber had been having a hard time at school and was still trying to make friends with a girl, who kept rebuking her for years. Just like me, (who had been trying to build bridges for years with my in-laws), Amber was attempting the same at school, to no avail. She had copied me. My strategy hadn't worked and neither had hers. I knew I had to set a bunch of new positive behaviours in motion for her to follow.

First, I had to change my perspective: I decided I could not change how people *behaved* towards me, but I could change *how* I responded, and what I *focused* on.

When we change our perspective on something, everything can change, just like that. From a space of necessity, where only I understood (or felt) what I was feeling as a mother witnessing the pain of her own child, I knew I only had one choice. I had to move out of the fear I was in and start to re-design my own sense of identity again.

Firstly, I would have to re-build my sense of self-belief in the aftermath of a painful and protracted divorce. Secondly, I'd have to think, behave and act as the best mother I could be, and lastly, I'd need to start seeing myself as a leader in my field, especially if I was going to create the necessary changes in the health and education systems, and live my life purpose. I would change those three perspectives: my own, my daughter's and then the world's, but it would start with how I saw myself. Having a new positive relationship with myself would create better relationships on the outside and I knew it, but I had to re-focus on who I was, who I wanted to be and the possibilities of what I could achieve in this life time.

I started by deciding that I wasn't going to worry anymore. I was going to *trust* that I was the best mother that Amber could have, and that I would step into that role. I would never from this moment on, let anyone compromise that goal or undermine it, regardless of what they thought of me. Then I made another decision: I was ready to get out there and teach again after six years. My Swiss mind-set coach, Niamh Kromo once asked me to question myself,

"What do I do, that would create the most impact for others, if I taught it to them?"

I knew what it was.

I had to show people my daily morning meditation practise and reach as many people as possible. If I did this online, I knew I could reach and influence people on a greater scale. I thought to myself that if only people knew the following fact that changed my life, they too would be able to easily change theirs:

When we wake up in the morning, what we *say* to ourselves and how we *feel* in the first five minutes of the day will set the tone for the whole day.

This is a fact, based on both teaching and personal experience; it changed how I organise my life and is one of the ways I have helped many reclaim their happiness.

The reason why a daily wake-up practise works for literally everyone is that 'waking up' is something we all do, every day! Learning how to create a hugely positive mental and emotional environment (at the start of each day) was how I developed my *Rise and Shine* learning model. I was certain that there was no-one on the planet who couldn't benefit from cultivating a habit that placed them in a space of pure daily connectivity with self from the second they woke up. Think about all the problems that would go away! You wouldn't worry about making the 'right' decision, you would just connect with yourself every day and follow your heart. In doing so, you would develop self-trust and the feeling of being divinely cared for. That feeling then leads to being unaffected by anyone on the 'outside' because their opinions and value systems would no longer be yours, instead you'd be cultivating, shaping and honouring your *own.* All your worries would start to fade, and you would learn to love yourself, step by step and make it more important than anything else. Reliance on money, medicine, drugs, alcohol, therapy, people or co-dependent relationships would surely become obsolete, because your focus would be on the self, and nothing in the material world would be able to match the good feelings of total self-trust.

Once you are fully in love with yourself again, by sheer practise of visiting yourself every day, you'll never want to put harmful things into your body or mind. It just won't 'feel' right. No one will ever be able to organise or control you again, because you'll be a self-governing entity! Imagine how that would feel? There is a reason some of the most consciously aware monks on the planet, remove themselves from society and sit with themselves on mountain tops, in silence or in nature. It doesn't seem so silly now, does it? They know that self-discipline, daily meditative practises and self-awareness create true joy, true awakening and honest spirituality.

For me, it was time to make this daily practise known. At the start of each day, I would show people that they can easily generate their own inner 'guru' and become truly free from the negative effects of the world.

5.2 - Going To Sleep

"Before anything else, planning is the key to success" – Alexander Graham Bell

When we go to sleep at night, what is in our minds will play out in our dream state and will affect how we feel when we wake up in the morning. That is why it is really important to ensure that when we go into sleep state, our minds are *clear* of worries, concerns and all negative energy accumulated throughout the day.

- We need to rest.
- We need to heal.
- We need to rejuvenate.

The mind is a very powerful engine that has been processing all day long, and I strongly believe that if we do not clear our minds before going to sleep, we can be negatively influenced by our own thoughts and the thoughts of those around us, which will set us up for the next day, where the cycle continues.

Think about it for a minute.

If the last thing you watch before you go to bed at night, for example, is the world news, what sorts of images and feelings will you take with you to bed?

Equally, if you have a challenging day at work and then go to bed without reconciling the situation, what do you think is going to play out in your sleep? How is that going to affect the way you feel the next day, and therefore how you perform in every area of your life?

Let's look at something that has become an epidemic in our society at the moment. If your mobile is 'dinging' with social media notifications before you go to bed, what are you feeding your mind? I am witnessing it in my own family and everywhere I turn. People are so glued to their "smart" phones that they are often sucked into "everything else" and lose sight of themselves and their own lives. The world's problems and dramas become your problems, and the mobile phone becomes an extension of the human arm. The focus is so cleverly external, allowing us to avoid our problems, deny ourselves attention and seek answers from society. The result is an increase in mental and emotional illnesses. Millions of children and adults today are plugged into things that fuel their anxieties. The "screen habit" is impacting on their sleep pattern, the things they watch is embedding into their brains, and the information overload is putting their whole wellbeing in jeopardy.

Aside the odd movie, I have chosen to not watch regular television since 1999. I don't watch the news either. I find it disturbing. I am mindful of how negative TV shows affected me when I was four. I had nightmares for years when I watched a horror film at an older friend's house, it kept me awake at night in fear of things that were not even real. I know you probably have one example of this in your own life and it is not a coincidence: what you put into your mind, whether it is what you see, read or buy into – becomes what you think about and drives your life. Suddenly, everything in your environment has the power and you don't. This is why it is essential to me that before I go to bed every night, I take some time to sit quietly and clear my mind in meditation. I need to empty the trash so that I am fresh for the next morning, otherwise it will spill over into the next day and affect the whole week. In the silence of my pre-sleep meditative practise, I can pinpoint anything that feels out of balance and I can resolve it, so that it does not follow me into the next day. I become my own therapist, because no one knows me quite as well.

Of course, meditating doesn't come easy for everyone. At the start, I too had to face the chattering mind which seems to never stop, and it was frustrating. This is why meditating must become a practise; with practise you always get *better*.

Many people I have spoken to can't get past the chattering mind, so never reach the depths of meditation and the blissful states that I frequently access as my norm. I can understand why. The mind is receiving information from so many different sources and frequencies constantly, that unless you have removed yourself from society for a bit, you think you are part of it, and it is a part of you. You have a hundred different voices in your head.

When I experienced my nervous breakdown in 2010, I did not look at my laptop for a year and my new iPhone sat in its box for a year too, untouched. I realise that for everyone, it is not always possible to be on your own and pull away from others. We as human beings need to interact. I just knew however that unless the connection with myself was strong, I wouldn't genuinely be able to connect with others. It was challenging not having anyone to guide me, but it served me beautifully, because I opened up to becoming my own guide and the voices of others, stopped. I got to face all the aspects of myself that I hadn't been facing because I was too busy being a character in someone else's story. I had been inauthentic to my own needs, and so I lived in fear. My energy became low and imbalances showed up in my mental, emotional, physical and spiritual body. I strongly believe that by mastering your emotional state, you will shed all the world's problems and see yourself properly for the first time. A really good sleep is one of the greatest ways to maintain a balanced emotional state and ensure that you never get overwhelmed.

If you are not sleeping properly, it is likely something is "on your mind".

If you want a clear head for the morning, or even a clear conscience: check in with yourself at night, the way you would do with an infant and nurture it to sleep by giving it some quiet and peaceful attention. This is one of the best ways to wake up fresh and ready to take the day on. Also, tuning into yourself before bed can bring great clairvoyant or insightful moments. Let me share one of my stories with you of something that happened to me in my moments before sleep; something that then manifested into reality. One night in 2010, before sleep, a strong yellow and blue colour appeared into my awareness. Now, I had been following the general election between the Conservative party ('Tories') and the Liberal

Democrats, who were campaigning in our area. I had been wondering who to vote for, and I had seen their signs up: Tories were blue, and Liberals were yellow. In my vision, both were equal, and I couldn't understand why I had received this insight. The very next day, I had a thought- we had a hedge outside my dad's house that would be perfect for putting up election sign-posts, so without thinking, I phoned both parties and said the strangest thing: I asked each party if they would like to put a sign up on the hedge and promote themselves and they were delighted. There was one clause though: they all had to understand that I was allowing *both* parties (blue and yellow) to campaign beside each other, and I let them know that I would be ringing the other party to offer the same deal. They accepted, and just like in my vision, yellow and blue were side by side outside the house. What happened thereafter was that after the general election was over, the two parties decided to combine forces and work side by side, forming the first ever Conservative-Liberal Democrat coalition policy. It was incredible. It doesn't matter to me whether I was shown this as a prophesy of what was to come, or whether I was shown it in order to take the action I did which prompted a new awareness- the only thing that matters is that if you follow any intuition you receive on the inside, you can see or create changes on the outside.

5.3 - What Happens in Between

How you wake up and go to sleep is the key to having a 'good' day every day, but what needs to happen in between waking and sleeping?

This a good question.

We act out a set of behaviours that are based on thoughts and emotions.

We do things to feel a certain way.

We make decisions every day without even realising it, based on our feelings.

The good news is this: If you have centred yourself in the morning and unwound your mind at night, you should be in the right thought-space to create behaviours and actions that benefit your day. When you begin by turning off all distractions and face yourself every day, you will always connect to what's *really* going on for you. It's about getting *real* with yourself, so that you can find balance in all areas of your life and show up every day as the strongest version of you. This will help you cope with whatever challenges crop up in between waking and sleeping.

Some of the changes you might make from doing this daily and nightly practise may alter your life experience. I have found that when you strip away everything in your life that may be interfering with your sense of happiness and face yourself, it can be both magical and painful. Do not let this dishearten you, because the truth is you were never truly happy anyway, if you were not in touch with yourself fully. It is not possible. This is especially true if you are venturing into new territories that other people who are close to you don't necessarily understand. Do people who *love* you want you to feel *bad*? It is unlikely. I have come to understand that if we rely on *anything* external to feel good, whether it is people or things...it's not genuine.

This is why systems are breaking down everywhere. Things that used to work, don't work anymore because we are outsourcing everything from tasks to advice. Luckily, this is causing people to wake up to new possibilities. Strangely, we are in a time of such technological and scientific advancement and yet we still have war, poverty and depravation. We are more aware and connected than ever and yet somehow less. Some things seem like they are going backwards, and we are moving away from what feels real. On Facebook, we are 'liking' everyone else's journeys, instead of focusing on our own true missions.

I'll give you an example: one of my absolute loves is music. I am a pianist and I used to spend hours playing the piano as a child. Remember when I said public speaking frightened me? Well, playing the piano never did. I seemed to get lost in the moment when I was playing and everyone else around me didn't exist until I had stopped. There were no thoughts, I just *played*. I practised and practiced and would be more than happy to perform. It was easy for me because I loved it. It was so exciting when I got through the pain barrier of learning new notes, rhythms, pieces and could play off-by heart for hours on end. Any chance that I got, I would play. Any chance I had to perform, I'd be there. It was pure joy.

That is, until I went to boarding school. I was allocated a new piano teacher, and because I was no longer at home, I lost the support of my mother who was my backup piano teacher, and who had nurtured my talent for years. I also had to get used to a new living environment away from my comfort zone and family, aged 11. I didn't connect with my new piano teacher and wasn't given another one that was more aware of my needs. At the same time, I was dealing with the news that I didn't get the music scholarship into my new secondary school, nor did I pass the exam to get in to Chethams; one of the most prestigious music schools in the country at the time.

Suddenly, I didn't want to play anymore.

Part of me had decided "I wasn't any good". The joy vanished. My early years of being an 'advanced' pianist were at an abrupt end. But how could I have been a great pianist and now I felt I wasn't? Then it hit me: I had been accustomed to the 'claps' and the feedback of my performances all through childhood, I had allowed myself to feel 'good', (because they had told me I was) and I defined myself as a great piano player because of that. But once something *else* cropped up on the other side of the fence, that told me I *wasn't* so good, I defined myself by that too. I had forgotten that I started to play the piano because I loved it, I was passionate about it *inside* and it was *me* at those keys, losing myself in the divine gift I'd been given.

This is the point: if your visions of what you can do (or be) are left in the hands of *other* people's choices or decisions, you will never have the power to win the battle of self-doubt when it arises to challenge you. Without *you* having *your* own back, there will never be enough external support to overcome the doubts that naturally creep in, especially when things 'go wrong'. You will 'fall asleep' back into the trance of disempowerment. If you want to support someone or be supported, support yourself first or your sense of empowerment won't last.

In fact, we can "wake up" and "fall asleep", metaphorically every day, if we do not master our own minds and emotional states in the morning and at night, which will guide us through those in-between times.

I feel strongly that as a global community, if we don't start listening to ourselves, we will fall short of our potential to perform at our greatest capacity as human beings and get completely lost in a noisy world that drowns out the most important inner guidance. As Brian Tracy once said, "If you do not have goals of your own, you will be doomed to live by the goals of others".

Chapter 6 - Rise and Shine

6.1 - It Takes 21 Days to Make or Break a Habit

They say it takes 21-days to make or break a habit in neurology. I remember hearing this in my leadership programme in 2008. During our training, we had been learning that when you release three significant emotional events that have been stored in the subconscious (and gain new positive perspectives), you immediately shift your awareness. This allows you to change life habits that may have been harmful (and created pain or lack) in some way. Whilst I had experienced changing lifetime habits overnight, I knew that if I could stick to any decision to change for 21 days, then it would be programmed in forever.

The first thing to realise when changing a habit, is that it is not as hard as you think to follow a new positive decision through. However, it only happens once you *decide* it is what you want. For example, I remember sitting in the doctor's waiting for my vaccinations before heading to India. I was reading a poster on the wall that said, "Thinking about stopping smoking? This may be the hardest thing you have ever had to do". I sat there and felt confused at these words, because it simply was not true in my experience. When I stopped smoking, it happened because I had made a sudden decision that I *wanted* to stop, because something deep inside of me was gnawing away at me. It had seemed so easy. But then I remembered the 13 years of thinking about stopping and how my internal battle over it was real. Part of me had wanted to stop and another part of me wanted to carry on. This went on for years. I didn't feel as healthy as I could be, and I had been ignoring my feelings that clearly said, "it's time to stop". It was very challenging because I did not know how to do it. It was a habit that had been controlling me for over a decade. I knew I wanted to stop but I didn't know when or how. A friend had simply told me, "you will stop when you are ready to stop, and you will know". These were wise words since they had been a smoker too. It didn't make it any easier, but what I did do was listen and read the book that they recommended – Alan Carr's *Easy Way to Stop Smoking*. I know for a fact that this hasn't worked for everyone because some are not quite ready to let go of a habit that is killing them. On some level, perhaps they don't feel worthy of love, for whatever reason.

For me, this book did work. It made me aware that I did not feel good about smoking, and that was the first time I knew I had to decide and finally act. I just stopped smoking overnight. I sat on the beach on a gloriously sunny, crisp January afternoon and suddenly I knew it was time. The excitement that welled up inside me was extraordinary. It was done. Like I said in a previous chapter, I had absolutely no withdrawal symptoms, just a feeling of great joy. This was in January 2004 when I began happily ticking off the dates in my diary as each day passed, ecstatic that every day I was choosing to be a person who no longer smoked.

Years later, I spoke to friends who had also battled with the nicotine habit. They shared with me that because they had seen me stop smoking so easily, they too had stopped smoking. I felt overjoyed to hear this, but I knew this wasn't going to be the case for everyone, some habits need a bit more work. One month after I stopped, I was asked by Rachel (the Reiki Master from whom I received a reiki attunement) to do a self-healing practise for 21-days and I just did it without question. This was simply placing my hands on my body in certain positions from my head to my feet, every morning and evening. It felt good. I was paying attention to myself. I was giving love to myself. Focusing my attention inwards in a simple, gentle way was keeping the good feelings flowing. As well as laying my hands on myself, part of the attunement process was to simply write down any awareness that presented itself to me during that time. In doing this consistently, it created a focused routine, some daily discipline and a point of reference to see how far I had come. Had I not written it all down, I would not have that record to refer back to.

My point is this. We are creatures of habit. We all develop and exercise habitual behaviour every day. Some of the things that we do hurts us or other people in some way, and sometimes we are not even aware of it. When we decide that it is time for change, I believe from my personal and professional experience, that there are no hard and fast rules in terms of the results that we can expect to achieve. But neurologically, if it takes 21 days to fully re-program a new way of consistent being into your system, then you must decide to take that action and see those days through regardless. It will give you physical evidence that you have changed your mind.

In 2008, I was introduced to the idea of 'accelerated learning'. This included reviewing anything new that you learn in an hour, 24 hours, a week and a month. I have included these principles in my daily practise and teachings to help anyone who feels ready to make a change. There is only so long that you can hide from yourself in my opinion, especially if you create a space of meditation. So, tell yourself that even if you kick a habit like I have - in one day or one week - that you will continue a process of change for at least 21 days, to avoid any relapse. Plus, when you strip away distraction and create that space to sit with yourself and simply identify how you are feeling to start with, that is where it all begins to work. Anything less than feeling "okay" requires attention. Sometimes we are not ready to face what that is. Sometimes we are not ready to make the changes. We can hide from ourselves by indulging in the very things that repress the uncomfortable feelings (like smoking drinking, medicating), but honouring how we really feel is the only way to take our lives to the next level.

If you are not feeling fulfilled, enriched, happy and joyous, then by sitting with that feeling every day, it is possible to cultivate a new habit of self-love and care. Consistently show up for yourself, enquire and take the actions necessary to break down habits that do not serve your highest good, and follow through on any insights that unfold from that space of silence and reverence.

It may take less or more than 21-days to make or break a habit for you but dedicate those 21 days in full to your recovery process just to instil new positive ways of being. With practise, it becomes easier.

I am able switch to new habits quickly because I choose self-love these days. I regularly take myself to a quiet space and sit with any feelings of discomfort that come up. I ask myself how I am feeling, I then ask the feeling what it would like me to know and then what I need to do about it.

Here is my daily process:

Start of day

- Sit with self before breakfast.
- First, identify how I feel.
- If it's uncomfortable, I amplify the feeling, however uncomfortable it is – I don't push it away, I connect with it instead. What's going on? I listen for the answer. It comes quickly for me, but it will come to you in whatever time it wants to take, so be patient.
- I ask the awareness what it wants me to know or pay attention to.
- Then, I ask myself what I need to do.
- I do an ecology check: Is taking this action good for me, my family, my community, the planet? I ask three times and if it is a yes, I trust it is a priority that needs addressing now.
- I ask myself when to take the action that is presented to me, I trust, and I do it without hesitation.

End of day

- I check in with myself before bed.
- Did I meet the intentions that I set in my morning practise?
- If yes, I acknowledge and celebrate quietly in my mind.
- If no – with no self-judgement, I accept this and ask myself what I will do differently next time.
- Who do I know that is really good at whatever it is I have identified that I need to do?
- What would they do? (model it)
- When will I do it?
- I make a firm commitment to myself to do it and I intend to take rapid action. I tell myself that "action creates traction". It builds confidence, momentum and the results in my life.
- I only take one step at a time to avoid overwhelm and I keep consistently moving forward, choosing one small step and one big scary step.
- I ask for support from someone who has already achieved what it is I need to do, especially if I have a gap in knowledge or skills in this area.

Due to this daily process, I have broken tons of disempowering or unhealthy habits such as the following:

- **(2004)** Smoking
- **(2009)** Stopped drinking caffeinated drinks for 9 years. No desire. No withdrawal.

- **(2011)** I left my marriage and did not look back. I got into a new habit of loving myself enough to put myself first and started living in a truly authentic way, where I could love myself back to full health.
- **(2012)** I quit all dairy products for about 3 years. I requested clarity on how to achieve optimum health during meditation. I was instructed to receive Kinesiology diagnostics which in turn identified dairy intolerance and so I stopped immediately.
- **(2013)** I became gluten free. Kinesiology diagnostics showed that I was gluten intolerant, so I stopped consuming anything which contained gluten until April 2017 when I tested as no longer gluten intolerant.
- **(2015)** I had not been planning my meals properly and so had been experiencing low energy. I decided to regain my balance through nutritious food. I cultivated the habit of daily food logging all meals, to identify what made me feel well and not well. I re-introduced foods into my system after being unable to digest gluten, dairy, meat, yeast, shell fish, sugar. It was amazing. I just carried on logging for two years, this led me to planning my meals instead of eating on the fly and feeding myself low nutrient foods to stave off hunger.
- **(2016)** I increased my hydration. I had not been drinking enough water and so I started logging it in my food diary to bring my awareness to it, and then set a specific target for increasing my uptake every day.
- **(2018)** I restarted gentle daily yoga practise every morning, once I felt that my ankle injuries could sustain something I had

once done for years. I passed the 21-day mark and now it is just what I do again. If I had not have kept it going, I might have let my ankle injury act as an excuse.

Currently, one of my focuses is on skincare, because I can forget to take care of my skin. I am holding myself accountable by setting a goal for 21-days to focus on it. I declared it in public online, and in a private Facebook group to increase accountability and support for my focus.

You see, after 21 days of ensuring you do something like this every day, it will become an automatic part of what you do.

If you want to set a new goal, you must:

- Decide what you want to create
- Believe you can have it
- Visualise having it
- Generate feelings of celebration inside even if you haven't achieved the result yet
- Amplify those feelings in your morning and evening meditations
- Journal – as an end of day practise, acknowledge all the 'wins' in the direction of what it is you have decided to achieve, and keep creating the evidence of your daily achievements.

Don't forget to ditch self-judgment when things don't go right. Be flexible, practical, find another way if you have to, and speak to someone who has already achieved what it is you wish for yourself. The consistency of these daily habits all come together to help you achieve the goals that you want. It's simple. Practising feeling *good* is the starting place for manifesting the things that you wish. You need to elevate your energy to match the frequency or vibration of what it is that you wish for yourself, and become it. So, for me, the priority is to cultivate the habit of how to feel good every day before breakfast and then do my utmost to bring this in to every aspect of my day before bed, where I cleanse and prepare for a new day.

When a day doesn't go right, I can come back to my end of day *Rise and Shine* meditation, check in with myself and come back into alignment before I go to sleep, so that I can clear up anything that may not have "flowed" during the day. I then decide before I sleep how I want to show up for myself when I wake up. I switch off and trust all is well.

Chapter 7 - When The Sh*t Hits the Fan

7.1 - Being Ahead of The Game

When I realised my marriage was falling apart and I needed to leave it, I understood that sometimes in order to get a clean, fresh start you have to walk through some crap first. So, what happens when sh*t hits the fan? Because it is likely that we will all experience things going in the complete opposite direction than we had planned, and we need to be ready for it.

In the last chapters, I explained that putting myself in the best possible emotional state every day, has allowed me to cope with the curve balls that life can throw. By sitting in meditation every day and continually developing the *Rise and Shine* practise, I have discovered a few things. I noticed that getting in touch with how I *really* feel every day and then honouring that truth by taking rapid action (on anything that is presented to me during that space), means life solutions appear continually.

This is particularly true when I face something that feels uncomfortable, and choose to do something about it anyway.

When the chips are down, being able to:

- put things into perspective
- stay resourceful
- remain in a state of peace
- keep smiling and problem solving

- find the lesson and the blessing

has helped me to navigate my life at the most challenging of times.

Similarly, when you are ready to:

- meet with your deepest self and become totally honest with how you feel
- explore what you want in this life
- take steps every day to create that in your world

Miracles can and do happen.

So, when sh*t hits the fan, in whatever form it may take shape, I know that it pays to be mentally and emotionally adaptable and resilient. These emotional muscles are strengthened daily when you come back to your core, feeing calm and in control. From here, you are best placed to tap into your wealth of inner resources and make decisions from an empowered space that can best serve you, your family and your community. Some of the best decisions I have made in life, have been from a place of personal calm and not fearful reaction. I had to face how unhappy I felt *first* and choose to love myself *more* than the fear of leaving any security, income, the unknown, and so on. Essentially, I was stepping into the void and trusting that it would take me where I needed to go. It was terrifying in some ways, but I knew it was the only way to do it.

What do you do when you are out of familiar territory, how do you feel safe? You use your *heart* as your most reliable compass. When you follow your heart and nothing else, all the practical matters are secondary, because you are honouring your truth, and your truth will never take you to a lie or into somewhere unhappy.

Recently in Cyprus, a friend who I had not seen for twenty-one years, was in the depths of his divorce process. He noticed that I was smiling as he talked to me and commented, "you are still in your bubble". I realised then that the thousands of hours of learning, coaching and meditating had been paying off. Even though seeing him was a staunch reminder of the depths of trauma that I had experienced during my divorce, he recognised that I had protected myself more than I had realised. I had not let the storm continue to rage but instead had let it pass through. Did that mean there were no more curveballs after my divorce? Of course not. Life is about growth and you can't grow without a little challenge to test your resolve. You don't need perfect external circumstances to stay composed *inside.* Feelings of fear will come but you just don't let them stay. The best way is to tune into your heart, tap into your truth and trust that all will be well.

This is why I advise my clients to wake up early and connect with themselves as soon as possible, before they make any decisions for the day. When you wake up at 5am in the morning feeling bright-eyed and bushy tailed, it feels energising and thrilling. Clarity and inspiration begin to flow once you do this daily, but there is another reason for this early waking that benefits your physical health.

In my early twenties, I used to be a party organiser. As much as this suited my free spirit at the time, it also meant that my body clock was upside down. Going to bed late and getting up late means you miss those sacred hours of the day, where you can align with yourself in silence. Once I realised that the party scene- even though it was fun- was harming my ability to think clearly and function properly during the day, I shifted my focus. I turned to self-healing modalities such as Reiki, yoga and became a mother – all in the same year - 2004. Since then, my daily practise has evolved and continues to do so. I kept growing, kept learning and adding to my skill set. In 2011, I began looking further into spiritual practises. At this time, I received 'Magnified Healing' through spirit master Quan Yin, and learned how to re-connect with the angelic realms alongside amazing spiritual teacher, Eloise Bennet.

In 2014, Eloise introduced me to a sacred geometry expert called Zlatko Kanda and I was able to communicate with archangel Metatron via a Sacred Geometry Healing attunement. This was significant as Metatron is the angel that governs over children and unknown to me, I was about to decide to go to court to discuss the fate of my daughter, Amber. I remember clearly at the time Zladko telling me that I would have to go through a "maze riddled with thorns", and court was exactly that. I was eventually awarded primary carer of my daughter and declared to be a fit mother, but since my garden of peace had been disturbed for such a long time (even before this drawn-out and painful event) it needed to be weeded, re-planted and nurtured.

The integration of my new teachings and my constant meditation on higher forms, opened up my awareness further. It shifted my consciousness and increased my intuitive abilities, allowing me to override the negative thoughts in my head when things didn't look so good. The thoughts in our mind can be like weeds and if they are strangling us, it's like the breath of life being squeezed out. It's constrictive, there is no flow and so all of your creativity gets interrupted. It is easy to put myself into this space of fear now from memory: my throat gets tight, I find it harder to breathe and my shoulder starts to ache as I feel myself disconnecting from my life source, or inner support network.

Now, the good news is, I can reverse this immediately. As I consciously focus in the opposite direction and imagine an infinite number of people reading my words and rejoicing as they learn how to navigate their mind, rediscover the wisdom in their hearts and tap into truth, I start to relax and breathe easily and effortlessly. I begin drawing light, life and hope into my cells, as I picture my readers doing the same. Now I am back into the present moment. If we do not learn how to let go of the past and master our minds, there will be no progress for any of us, and life will just be painful. The only way to let go of the past is to face it first, because it will always come back until we have paid attention to what it needs to heal, learnt from it and allowed ourselves to grow past it. Of course, sometimes growth can be painful too but at least it is pain that will move you forward, not keep you trapped. I write these words to you with Mother Mary's guidance.

In 2014, my growth came by accepting that I could no longer process my divorce without some knowledge. That is when I decided to take it to court and trust that it would work out. My life felt like it had become part of someone else's game; a game that I did not understand, because I was not playing one. After two years of failed mediation and ostracization by most of my in-laws, I felt that the negative impact on me and my daughter had been enough. I just couldn't do it alone anymore because I was devoting all my energy to my daughter, whilst experiencing no co-operation and important practical matters were getting on top of me.

I had finally had enough.

I had to take this to court and find a way through it.

I had to get ahead of the game. More than that, I had to trust I'd made the right choice even though I hadn't a clue what I was doing.

7.2 - Preparation Is Everything

I knew I had to prepare. Life felt torturous and it was confusing. It was time to get back on track and end this once and for all. I often wondered how could a simple decision to honour my truth and leave my marriage evoke such a negative response from other human beings? I didn't fully get it at the time.

My happiness was my business but if anyone thought it was a simple decision, they were wrong. It was extremely painful. In fact, it had taken me years to finally leave. My husband and I had values that were increasingly different, and the more time we spent running a business together and bringing up a child- I saw us drifting. I still loved my husband but something inside told me over and over again that it wasn't meant to be, it had taken me as far on this path as I would go. When I left, I knew it would be hard, but I didn't bank on how hard or anticipate the reactions I would get. I kept asking myself: Where's the rule book in divorce that says people have the right to create drama around someone else's pain? What was the point in that? How does it help anyone? Especially, the child involved.

So, of course the thoughts and worries that kept emerging inside me were horrific, as I could not get any conclusion from a set of mute people who were also key influencers in our daughter's life. I felt ill and tired. I knew the divorce could have been cleaner, less dramatic for her, but no-one seemed to see it the way I did. I was unable to move back into my own home with our daughter which was near my family, near her school and near my income stream. I had attempted an amicable relationship, but it was dwindling by the day and I had to break the legal contract of our business union too. Two and a half years of exhausting U-turns with little conclusion had drained me and I simply wanted to move forward, re-build my life and re-start my coaching business, from where I had left off in 2010.

My ex-husband appeared to be in intense pain when the paperwork came through to say that we were officially divorced, even though I had felt divorced for years, because of the strides I had already taken to separate and move on. I'd left our marital home, changed my name back to my maiden name but when reality hit for my ex-husband with the official writing on the paper, I felt that things got worse. I wasn't ready for it. I had moved on so far in my own mind, through my decisions and actions, that I had not factored in what happens when reality finally hits the other, who has not moved on. I felt I was witnessing someone's grief and pain becoming so insurmountable for them, that it was now coming out as threats or toxic remarks to me. I decided I wasn't prepared to be on the brunt of it any longer, because I knew my decision was best for everyone long-term. I realised they just couldn't see that yet.

Like I mentioned before, what would I have been teaching our daughter if I had stayed any longer in a marriage that no longer felt fulfilling? I had stayed long enough, trying to work it out to the best of my ability. Now I knew I had to prepare for a new path. My next step was a detox retreat in Glastonbury with colonics to help kick start my digestion, accompanied by regular kinesiology, nutritional coaching sessions, a weekly massage and reiki, daily yoga and weekly Pilates classes. This self-focus to get physically strong, coupled with my daily practise of self-enquiry allowed me to plan. I had to be ready for what was fast becoming the next necessary step. I had to be prepared for the court proceedings. I knew it would be my last step to end this battle even if I had no idea what to expect, or what the outcome would be. I had never believed that it would be necessary to go to court. How could I best prepare for the unknown?

Firstly, I called a judge that I knew, highly experienced in divorce law, and luckily someone who had also been through divorce himself. He pointed me in the right direction because he had seen it all before. My next inner guidance was, “Find yourself a good solicitor”. I walked into our local solicitors and met Emma, my appointed solicitor and explained everything I was going through. I felt relieved to have an objective voice; one who could help me understand the legal boundaries of my situation, and who also had Amber’s well-being at the forefront of her mind. When I went home, I continued to sit in my daily meditative practise and I followed the guidance on what to do next. I requested that my heart, my trusted team of angelic and ancestral guides and the energy of the universe, would allow the court outcome to be for the highest and greatest good of all. I then let go of *any* expectation of what that outcome would be. With the court taking care of all the practical details, I had more space to restore my energy and re-focus my attention fully on the jobs that I needed to continue to do, which were:

To be the best mum I could be and to get back out there to reach the minds and hearts of people by bringing in new helpful systems and practises.

To be in peak mental, emotional and physical shape and maximise support as best I could in every direction.

And finally, to have time to tap into my truth in meditation and keep following my heart.

I had to keep coming back to my own truth to shine a light on the next step. Part of that process was forgiving anyone treating me badly and forgiving myself for anything that I had said or done - consciously or unconsciously- to hurt anyone in the process. I had to stay calm in order to best manage my responses, in case any future anger was going to come my way. Fortunately, the fact that I had to deal with some horrible backlash actually deepened my ability to navigate my mind, emotions and internal responses. I knew if I kept facing the problems and working through them, I'd get better and better at it until outside circumstances only had brief negative effects on me. In other words, all your 'bad' experiences will lead you to another level of self-mastery. They allow you to be totally honest with yourself, about who you are and what you stand for. They produce the opportunity to stay strong in your resolve when nobody else understands where you are coming from. For me, sticking to my guns, even if it's made me unpopular in the eyes of my own flesh and blood was eye-opening. It helped me to follow through on what I believed to be true, no matter what.

I had to be prepared to be able to speak my truth and hold my ground, no matter what was thrown at me.

My life and my daughter's life depended on it.

7.3 - Plan It, Do It, Review It

I can remember sitting in a tent in a field in West Wales on Amber's 9th birthday: it was August, 2004. The sky was pouring with rain and I'd managed to pull another birthday party out of the bag somehow, despite the situation between me and my ex-husband reaching its breaking point. Legal professionals had warned me, "Cut contact with him now, you don't need to tolerate any more of this". I felt my heart sink. It was Amber's birthday and somehow, for her sake, I wanted us both to be there. As required, I had updated my solicitor with the outcome from our mediation session the same week, where we had agreed for Amber and her father to meet, but certain details of his past behaviour had come to light, and both the solicitor and judge had said Amber wasn't to see him until the case was resolved. I'm not sure how Amber felt. All I knew was that despite trying to pull out all the stops to make this party as fun as possible, I felt sick. In fact, I was physically sick, and it definitely wasn't from eating too much cake!

Earlier, I had packed my car up, and filled it with food that I could eat (which wasn't much). My digestion was failing because of the level of stress I was contending with. The latest challenge to deal with, was that I had been unable to move back in to my own house with Amber, after a U-turn on a mediation agreement that effectively left us homeless. We had gone to stay with my parents at their farm house. This was not ideal, because the level of stress that I was feeling was beyond challenging and I did not want it to seep out and impact my family. Today, I borrowed a tent and pitched up with a friend, her children and another friend in a campsite on a nearby cliff top campsite. I had decided to keep my word. The birthday plan with Amber's friends, some of mine and some of my family was going ahead, regardless.

I'd put up Leah's bell tent, which she had kindly lent me to host a classroom of Amber's friends. I'd arranged henna tattoos for everyone, and the children had been transfixed by the beautiful drawings on their arms. One after the other they had lined up. My friend Angela had brought in the most beautiful heart shaped home-made brownie cake and we'd all been playing rounders and hula-hooping. You see, I had planned to have a beautiful birthday celebration with Amber, no matter what. Things had escalated by now though between me and Matt, who was now officially my ex-husband. Final divorce paperwork had arrived, emotions were running high and I'd followed through, finalising the dissolution of our marriage. I was getting more and more concerned at how this would affect Amber. Firstly, by her witnessing the tension and also by how challenging it was to bring myself back to my centre and stay in a space of compassion towards certain people who had decided to become abusive. I had very little outside support at this time, so as usual, I followed my heart. It's all I had. My feelings were my navigator about how to take each next step and most importantly, I followed through every time. I kept Amber in the loop, promising myself I would never lie to her and explained what was happening from different perspectives. I wanted to help her get through what felt like an impossible and unbearably painful situation for all of us.

Once everyone had left the field and the party was over, I needed space and time to think. I reflected outside my tent, with the rain pouring outside and the words came to me:

"Plan it, Do it, Review it".

These words were engrained in me from my management training days.

I had adapted and incorporated this idea into my own daily practise and if there was a time when I needed to be able to tap into something to help me through this period of my life, now was the time.

I had to obey my own truth and trust myself beyond a shadow of a doubt. I had followed through on the party, I had taken legal advice and I had trusted my own inner wisdom to keep moving forward with no home, and no business. I could do the little things; make a small plan, follow it. Make another. This faith was how I would get through the next phase.

7.4 - Faith Is All You Need

What happened next was a God-send. My friend kindly offered me her static caravan to stay in for a few weeks and give me space to work out a long-term plan. I was so grateful for this breathing space, however moving into a tent, I now felt like I had nothing left except myself, the love of a few good friends, my parents and daughter and more importantly, my connection with the divine.

When you hit rock bottom, you must find your faith. Faith in yourself.

I had nothing so there was only one thing that I could do. Stay true to myself, do my daily practise, seek guidance from my heart and from the divine, and keep my faith that I was doing the right thing. I had discovered through diligently connecting with my heart and the divine in my daily meditative practise for years, that it is possible to elevate yourself to spaces which transcend the limitations of the mind. A place of deep peace. I had to have faith that the words that were coming to me in my meditations now needed to be followed, and trust that there was nothing to fear.

I had tried it the 'normal' way and it was now time to hand things over to a greater power to gain resolution and move on to walk forward into the next chapter of my life, with no regrets, a clear conscious and an open heart. My daily practise was (and still is) the key to continually finding faith in myself and moving forward in the most positive way possible.

As perceived challenges popped up in my awareness, I would deal with them in my mind and create strategies to overcome them. When your life feels like it has turned upside down and you have no-where to go, it's not true, it just *looks* true.

You always have one thing left: you have *you.*

There are resources buried deep within each and every one of us that we can tap into help us see *anything* through. I had faith in me. I had faith in the words that were coming through to me from a space of peacefulness every day. I was accessing greater wisdom than the fearful thoughts that would pop into my mind and I decided to keep searching for the clarity that would lead me to a new decision, a new action and a new result.

You won't always see how everything is so perfectly timed and designed to show you something profound until you have faith and follow your heart. Do you remember in an earlier chapter I told you that one night I just suddenly believed I was going to die – that I had two minutes to live and said 'goodbye' to everyone in total acceptance? While writing this book years later, I came to realise that life had been preparing me for the future. When I moved out of my marital home and across the road to my parents (a cross-road!), I realised the voice that told me "soon you'll be on the other side" was prophetic. I had indeed crossed over to the 'other side', both geographically and metaphorically, by leaving and starting a 'new life'.

These little signs will be revealed to you also if you realise that everything is going to have a purpose and a meaning, you just have to wait and have faith to see the bigger picture.

Chapter 8 - Celebration

8.1 - Celebration is The Key

No matter what you go through, you cannot spend your life dwelling only on the challenges. When you alter your focus, you will find that there is always something to *celebrate*, even in the most challenging of times.

For instance, as I write these words I can think of many memories; some are sad, and some are happy, but I know I can find a reason to pick out the ones for celebration.

This attitude of looking for the positive in all things is a really nourishing way of living. Even the things that are seemingly 'bad' memories have been times that I had the opportunity to grow, and I congratulate myself for having moved through them. Part of the process of bringing myself back into a place of balance after my nervous breakdown, was diligently writing three things down every morning that I felt deep heartfelt gratitude for in my life. It's part of my daily practise and has been for over a decade. It sounds simple and yet the best things in life often are. If we cultivate a sincere 'attitude of gratitude' in our life, it keeps us in our power to keep noticing all the things that are going right. Without thankfulness in life, what have we got? What are we left with?

For instance, I start with the smallest things. I am grateful to be alive. I woke up this morning when some people didn't – that's a miracle. I am also capable of so much: I can smile. I have free will. I can be unstoppable in my desire to live a true and meaningful life; doing what I love and helping to bring that joy to others. I celebrate simple tasks by acknowledging at the end of the day, I have achieved what I set out to achieve. We can often be so focused on the next task that we need to do, that we forget to take stock of all the little things that we created (and are creating) every day. Sometimes it is good to stop, take in the present moment and equally reflect on what we have accomplished that week. Simply being able to show up and choose to feel *good* is something worth celebrating, especially when things could feel tough and it does not need to involve anyone else – just you.

I strongly believe that practising a daily habit of gratitude, and then celebrating small victories nourishes our soul, and helps us to perform at our best. This shines through us from the inside out, into everything that we do.

When I set my daily goals in my morning practice before breakfast, I choose how I will celebrate the achievement of it. During the day, I enjoy trying to find ways to generate the feelings of celebration. It is one of my focus points as I move through my day, and it gives me the energy and motivation to complete things when distraction (or the unexpected) appears – which, as you know, can be a lot! We can all get distracted, can't we? Especially if we are not clear about what we are aiming for or are focusing on all the wrong things that do not add value to our daily experience.

Imagine what it would be like, believing in yourself so much that you continually know you will complete the goals you set for yourself? The ones that inspire you to jump out of bed in the morning feeling energised, motivated and great about life? Gratitude for everyday things is the quickest way to start the ball rolling on these feelings of consistent joy. For example, on the days where I feel like I am swimming through soup, I sit, connect with myself in silence, and pay attention to my thoughts and feelings. I become aware of how my body feels. Sometimes it is uncomfortable, because that is just the way it is. Then, I find something to *celebrate.* I start with something from my past, my current life or what I believe I am going to achieve or have, even if it's not there yet, and suddenly, I realise that things are good for me. It's not so bad when you are focused on all the good memories or dreams. Mostly, I find a way to celebrate life, because no matter what happens – being alive is the greatest gift of them all.

If you know me personally, you will know that I spontaneously dance down the street, on a train platform, on a beach, wherever. I put my head phones on and I begin celebrating the music of life, without a care in the world. I always feel connected to much more than myself, I know I am part of a universe that is in constant flow, and I flow with it. This is life that we all have the opportunity to participate in if we stop caring what people think of us. This starts with a belief that we have the right to joy. In my world, life is more sacred than opinion, it is worth living and we are all here for a reason. We are not supposed to be creating struggle, strife and war.

That comes from focusing on all the things we think we want to have and have to take from others. It is time to focus on *self.* The reason why each of us are here and the excitement of what that might be. That in itself is worth celebrating, don't you think? We are all unique in some ways, but we can all do similar fundamental things:

- We all think.
- We all feel.
- We all want to achieve something.
- We all want to be loved.

When we find the love in ourselves and realise how truly magnificent we are, nothing can touch that. I tune into myself every morning and evening in meditation and give myself that love. In my experience, when you can unlock the wisdom of your heart by the simple act of listening, the doors to the universe truly open. I have discovered the treasures buried deep inside the chambers of my heart and unlocked many a riddle from my journeys into that space. Because of this, I get to see life as truly magical in so many ways. I notice that each and every day we have in this wonderful world, is worth celebrating and I do this consciously because what we focus on *grows.*

Where our attention goes, energy flows.

What would happen if you started to notice the small things that require celebration, every day for the rest of your life? How do you think you would see, sense and feel life then? You can hardly feel terrible if your focus is on love.

When the chips are down, you can still dig deep inside and find something to feel grateful for and then celebrate it in some way. This will turn your world around in a matter of minutes and allow you access to resources you never knew you had.

8.2 - Driving Yourself Is Not The Way

How often do you sit with yourself, to simply be with *you*?

People are so afraid of being alone, never realising that it is not true. You have yourself always. I stripped away lots of people to get back to the real *me*, and to get comfortable with myself. It's been a journey and a half, but when there are no more reasons and excuses left to not do the things in your life every day that light you up, where else is there left to go? That is something for me to feel grateful about: when people let me down and I had to retract into my own being, I found my heart and soul. There were no more distractions, no more running away or running towards anyone or anything.

Have you ever avoided yourself and not even realised you were doing it?

I did in the early days.

When you become totally real with yourself about who you are, and there are no more illusions or distractions, it can feel absolutely terrifying. When we are so fixated on clinging to the things, people or situations that we think we need in life, it can become a torturous and vicious circle of pain. I know, I've been there. Letting go of the beliefs and conditioning that we are not even aware are driving our subconscious behaviours is quite daunting, especially when we as human beings are not aware of the influences that have shaped and formed us, all of our lives. One simple negative belief that we refuse to let go of can impact our lives in the most devastating way for years, without being aware that our health, relationships or careers are showing up in a mediocre or dissatisfactory way as a result.

How do you know that is you? Your life will feel unfulfilling in some way, and if it does and you tune into those feelings with patience, your heart will tell you why.

Connect with yourself each day, and find out what key belief about yourself is holding you back in some way from fulfilling your potential. You should not be dragging yourself from bed, but rather jumping out of bed every day, feeling energised, excited and blessed to have the opportunity to engage with life for yet another day.

Where do these beliefs come from that we have to settle for less than what we feel is absolutely true for us?

Are they *our* beliefs or are they someone else's?

We believe that our beliefs are ours, but ingrained beliefs tend to come from our parents, siblings, friends, schools, religions, the work place, media, politics, society...and so on. They shape us without us even knowing it, and they become a part of who we are. A good way to override this external influence is to tune into our own value system. A value is something we deem important to us, and it can be a good driving force behind new behaviour. Have you considered what is important to you in the context of your health, your career, your relationships and your life recently? What happens if you don't take time to consider what is important to you in all areas of your life, and take steps to align yourself with your own truth? The answer is that you'll end up living your life through the beliefs and values of *someone else.*

For example, I told you music has always been important to me. In the past, I became part of the music and events industry because I thought that was a good outlet. However, when I got really clear on what I wanted for me, I realised that I could no longer attach myself to a music industry that supported the recreational drug scene. It was a slippery slope and there were other more empowering ways for me to honour my love of music. Knowing my values also helped me leave my marriage, against all logic. I knew that I wanted to be with someone who was fully aligned with my truth, my values and my search for true, unconditional love. If I stayed, I would be 'OK' but not living up to the deepest desires of my heart and soul. If you have a wakeup call to the fact that your values are so misaligned with your marital partner and almost lose yourself in the process of keeping them happy, then really ask yourself if that 'lie' is best for all?

That is why I had to leave and if you are going through the same thing – do not care about how it looks, but how it *feels*; just listen to your inner guidance.

In meditation, there is nowhere to run. When you have the courage to hear your thoughts or feelings enough, you'll be finally prepared to do something about it. What really matters is learning the lessons when you are ready to receive them. You must focus on how you can grow from every experience without bias, and let go of *anything* that could harm you or anyone else in the long term. Some say that we are spiritual beings having a human experience, and some believe that we are doomed to stay stuck in our spiritual growth until we learn whatever we are supposed to learn. If either of these are true, then the outside world comes *second.*

Since I can't change what others choose to believe about me because that is their business, I focus only on what I can change about me.

Don Miguel Ruiz's wisdom springs to mind again as it is so important.

"Don't take anything personally".

He tells us, *"Nothing others do is because of you. What others say and do is a projection of their own reality, their own dream. When you are immune to the opinions and actions of others, you won't be the victim of needless suffering".*

I know this is sometimes difficult to do but mastering this ability is a huge step into true freedom. My journey is always about finding the higher perspective, no matter what people say about me or do to me. When I feel abused or affected by the outside world, I tell myself there was clearly something in me that attracted that experience in for a reason. There must've been something in that interaction that I needed to "get", and when I do, I learn a valuable lesson that stops it from happening again.

What is important is that these people came into my life for a reason and I thank them quietly for showing up to teach me something new about myself.

For years, I had often been driving *myself* with my eyes wide shut! I crashed and burned when I put my mind in charge, and yet every time I handed the wheel to the divine energy that comes to me in meditation-the one that has my very best interests at heart- I always knew I'd be doing the right thing for me.

When you invest your energy into someone else's vision, when you let that be your driver – you will drive yourself into the ground.

If this has been *your* experience, the only thing left to do is:

- STOP
- Re-evaluate by tuning back into the values of your heart
- Create a new plan based on that new information.

For me it involved putting *myself* back into the centre of my own life!

Is that selfish?

No, it's not.

It's the most unselfish thing you can do because it is being truthful.

When you fill your own cup up first, through authentically meeting your own needs in an ecological way, every day, I truly believe that you are then best placed to serve others.

I have discovered that when you become absolutely clear about what is going wrong in your life, it's a great time to re-design and create the life you truly want. One that feels amazing, enriching and enchanting. You must tap in to the truth of what lights you up.

8.3 - Trust In The Flow

As I write these words, I am sitting alone. I am surrounded by pieces of my past, my present and no doubt- my future. Just like you. In my mind, the only thing that is real however, is what is happening *right now*.

It's all in your mind: your past, present and future.

Fortunately, your mind does not know the difference between imagination and reality. This means you can change perspective on *every* memory you have ever had.

Why is this important?

We all have the capacity to set ourselves free from every thought and memory that we ever had, so that we can live fully in the present moment, and create futures for ourselves that are beyond what we may have thought was previously possible. For example, right now

I am consciously in flow, connecting with you in this moment, surrounded by a support team of invisible guides. I can feel their presence and yours. My heart lights up as I recognise and share this fact.

It's my truth and I live by it.

There was a time that I would not have shared this. My ex-in-laws were labelling me 'bi-polar' during my breakdown, and the pamphlet in the mental health building had advised that talking to angels or feeling like you are on a mission were symptoms of that very disorder. How dangerous is that?

Well, I do communicate with angels and they with me. I am also on a mission.

My mind is free, and my heart is pure because of it.

No matter what culture, religion or social background you are from, whether you know me personally or not and whether you are a direct blood relation to me or not, we all have something in common. We are all connected in some way through the very fact that you were ready to read my words and that you are right here, now, in this moment reading them.

Just think about it.

I don't know if you will realise by the time you finish reading this book, or whether you have already realised it, but we are the same you and I, regardless of what we practise. These words that I am writing, simply come through me, with no thought attached to them. I speak my truth without fear and it has taken a lot of courage to be myself in this way. I have discovered that doors open easily for me when I listen to the wisdom of my heart every day, trust the flow and act on it. This will work for you too. I also know that when you are in flow, time seems to stop and there is nothing really to think about, you just relax.

Take a moment now to consider the things that you have done and currently do in your life where time feels like it stands still.

Where there's just nothing. No fears, no flooding thoughts, just deep peace and total bliss. Just BEING. You can access this too at any time if you sit with yourself and just *be*, because if I can, anyone can.

The first two chapters of this book were written in Cyprus. It took a while to write each section, but I simply trusted what came through my fingers, let it go and moved on to the next section. I then started to feel unwell. I sat in meditation and sought guidance. I awoke at 3am, got my journal out and received my answer. The answer was this:

"To become well again, go home."

"When?" I asked. "The next flight home", was the response.

My friends asked me to stay, my mind thought it was too random but as always, I knew I was tapping into something that was beyond my conscious understanding and that I must follow this truth. This is what happens when you live in the flow. I had trusted my guidance in meditation to go to Cyprus eight months earlier to write my book and now, I was packed up and heading home to Wales, which is where this book wanted to be finished. I found myself in the same environment that I felt I had to leave during my painful divorce. I needed these feelings to rise up in me in order to write chapters five to eight. To express the truth of my experiences meant I had to allow myself to *relive* them, to feel the pain of the past again. I then used some Neurolinguistics re-patterning, visualisation and Magnified Healing to take myself back through my timeline and receive a new perspective on the memories that still exist in my system. This allowed me to move through it. By following what my heart told me, I was healing parts of myself deeply. I used Metatronic Sacred Geometry and Seraphim Healing to clear, heal, activate & harmonise my chakras. I also focused on my mental, emotional, physical, spiritual and etheric bodies, my DNA and cells to integrate my higher self in to my system.

The *Rise and Shine* process also helped me to set my daily intention and action steps, and to clear any subconscious fears about writing this book.

Trusting in the flow is easy, when you know what it feels like. You start to realise with practise that when you are not in flow, it will feel excruciatingly painful. All that means is you have not been listening to your inner voice of wisdom and acting upon it. It means that you have been listening to the fears and limitations of *others* who project their truth onto you, but that is their truth, not yours and you do not have to take it on. Defining how you wish to live your life and actually acting on it daily are two totally different things, but you will not act if you don't trust in yourself. When I tap into truth, it always goes way beyond my conscious understanding, that's how I know it is real. I am always presented with wisdom and strategies that I have not learned in this lifetime.

When you align yourself with your truth and take committed action every day in the direction of your dreams, you can't go wrong. There's always hurdles, it's just the way it goes but it should never stop you, it is just a test to see how much you want to listen. I find ways to move through my fears or lack of knowledge when something comes up, so that I can keep moving. I have heard that some people struggle with trying to understand what their life purpose is, but I believe that the answer lies deep within each and every one of us.

When you are on track, living it, you will know anyway because it will *feel* right. You'll just know.

8.4 - Creating Space

One day, I was in an art gallery in West Wales, surrounded by the beauty of Sarah Jane Brown's exhibition. When I saw the title of the exhibition, I couldn't believe it.

She had called it, *Creating Spaciousness.*

This was a phrase that had been one of the focuses of a six-month training programme called **P.E.R.F.O.R.M.** that I had designed for entrepreneurial women.

Sarah had been a participant. She came over once she noticed me looking around and whispered in my ear, "Go and take a look at all the names on the paintings". I gasped. They all represented 'lightbulb' moments that had popped up for her during our coaching sessions. Sarah had interwoven them into her art-work. No words can describe what I was seeing and experiencing in that moment.

As I read the names of each piece of art, the images in her paintings fused, and I experienced a kind of trance that cannot be put into words. My six-month program for women had come to life in front of me. I hadn't let anyone in on what PERFORM meant until the last day:

Practicing

Enlightenment

Restores

Faith and

Overcomes the

Restless

Mind

This is also the underlying mantra to *Rise and Shine*. However, do you find that often you don't realise what you are learning or the magnitude of it until after the event?

Well, you can only see the importance of things happening for you in real time, when you create space for yourself every day. Practising enlightenment and tuning into the greater network of the universe, instead of simply the network of people you are used to, helps to navigate and overcome the restless mind. It brings up and clears past memories that still generate fear by accessing the wisdom of your heart, which tells you there is nothing to fear.

Einstein once said that, "You cannot solve a problem with the same thinking that created it". This is true. Whether you believe me or not, your standard thinking in the past has not always served you, and maybe it is time to try something new; something more *profound*. If every problem is a problem of the mind, then every problem can be solved with the mind. The difference is you must tap into a greater mind. Opening up to all magical possibilities is *freedom*.

Now you may be wondering what the title of the book F.R.E.E.D.O.M. means, as you have almost come to the last section of this book. The truth of the matter is, it can mean anything you would like it to mean. I know that may seem frustrating because people like to see things set in stone, but that is exactly where you get stuck and stop playing with life. You see, tomorrow it may mean something else for me or you, because it depends on what is going on in your life. What would you like FREEDOM to mean to you? Today, for me, FREEDOM means:

Fearlessly

Restoring

Energetic

Escapes and

Demystifying the

Overcrowded

Mind

Tomorrow, I may change it. As the path moves, so do I. As the guidance changes, I follow. That is how it works. That is what being in flow *is,* always moving forward. I like acronyms, they are easy to remember and fun to play with. One time, when I listened and acted upon my truth during meditation, I received the programme "Create Your Perfect W.E.I.G.H.T". Kinesiologist Lise Matthews, Nutritionist, Amy Desborough and I put our skills together, and created a programme around this and it was an incredible experience. On the final day of that programme, I shared what 'WEIGHT' meant at that time:

When

Everything

Integrates

Great

Happiness

Talks

You must remember how to play again and go with the flow. Isn't it time that we offered some peace to ourselves, laughed more and stopped the negative nonsense-thoughts that rob us of moment-to-moment joy?

My mission is to create world peace one person at a time, and I can do it when I take it one step at a time. I want to teach people how to empower themselves without medication and show them their greatest and quickest healer – the built-in self-help systems in the body, mind and heart. All you must do to begin, is create some space in your mind to know that you are already perfect, and that you have wisdom inside you that is your ultimate truth. Live by this every day, and you will grow to have absolutely no doubt in your own abilities, just clarity, as you watch unlikely and magical things unfold in your life. When you live by your truth in a heartfelt way, with full responsibility for your own life with no shame, blame or judgement towards yourself or anyone else, then you are *free*. It's simple.

Just wake up every day and promise yourself you will visit the 'real' you, you will talk to your heart, you will listen and most of all you will act on the instructions it gives with fearless courage. Do the same in preparation for the next day, and no matter what you've been through, you will *Rise and Shine* every day in complete blissful alignment to the inherent magic of your heart.

Chapter 9 - From My Story to Your Story

Leaving the past behind, dropping things that no longer served me and focusing only on my higher purpose and truth has been painful; this book has shown that on many occasions. Was it worth it? Absolutely. One of the most exciting things about freeing yourself, tuning into your divine wisdom and showing up for yourself and others with integrity every day, is that soon people start to be magically affected by your energy. What then happens is, they want to live *their* truths too and grow out of the subconscious prisons that have kept them feeling less than perfect. Following your vision is not selfish, because it changes the world around you.

Through my coaching and the *Rise and Shine* process, I know that I can affect people's lives for the better, because I am lighting a path to the wisdom, truths, and freedom of others. All they ever needed was a daily structure that kept them focused and lit up inside in a consistent way. My clients and friends know my *Rise and Shine* process well, and I am so fortunate that a selection of them have decided to share their experiences and stories with you in this final chapter. I include these 'success' stories below for two reasons:

Firstly, it shows me everything I have trusted in and shared with you in this book *works*, and the gratitude I feel to be able to affect the lives of others in this way has no words. Secondly, it shows *you* (the reader) some solid evidence of the *power* of doing a daily practise, no matter what you have created up until now. If you just start where you are at, you can begin to raise your own bar of expectation and open up new space to feel enriched, empowered and nourished every day.

It hasn't been easy to open up about my own past, but I hope that it provides some hope and comfort that no matter where you are in life, if you just listen to your heart, it will never lead you astray and you can create anything you desire from this moment on.

I want to thank *you* the reader for coming on this journey with me. You may know me, or you may not but in this book, I have attempted to explain how my process, my coaching and my beliefs have come to be; I wanted this book to be the precursor to who I am *now,* to show you that I didn't just wake up one day fulfilled or divinely guided, it took *work*. The work however is the most worthwhile work you will ever do, and I want to thank the beautiful people below for honouring that work and making the commitment to change their lives:

Patricia Agnew- Former UN Staff and Reflexologist

In my mid-60s and after big life changes, Rachel supplied the knowledge and support to help me stay 'on top'. Working with Rachel means well-balanced insightful support, combined with a deep knowledge of individual needs. It is never boring, and the result is stability through regular teachings within the *Rise & Shine* programme.

Meditation provides a balanced approach to life's strings & arrows. The routines of morning and evening group meditation 'online' creates a sense of belonging for anyone who is looking for sound approaches/teachings, from someone who understands and practices the benefits of group work and regular installation of meditative practices.

Nick Otten - Landscape Gardener and Tree Surgeon

Rise and Shine has been a profound, progressive opening which has helped me clear the blocks for an exciting new life, in which I am empowered and free. I am sovereign in my world. Yay!!

Miranda Betts – Singer/Songwriter

Working with Rachel was a fantastic experience. I learnt such a lot about myself, as well as some really helpful techniques for setting goals and reaching them. The *Rise and Shine* programme quite literally changed my life! I set myself a seemingly impossible goal; to give up smoking after 30 years. And.... I did it! Rachel is both dynamic and inspiring. Her love of life is infectious, and she is a great teacher. Patient and kind and always willing to find solutions;

I have no hesitation in recommending her and her programme to anyone, but especially to those who are ready to make a change in their lives (but who need some extra help and support to achieve this.) Learning to include a daily practice in my life -however short- has helped enormously. I now carry this learning into my everyday life, and am so glad that our paths crossed, and I found this wonderful teacher.

Michael Jones – Support Worker (for adults with learning disabilities)

I love working with Rachel because when I am aided by her enthusiasm and confidence, I know that there is a greater meaning to life and that we all have so much potential. I have been able to find greater depth in myself. I now know I am here for a reason and life is so much more exciting. I have more determination to find my core spiritual connection, and be the person I was born to be. Rachel's enthusiasm is infectious. She has helped me take responsibility for myself rather than feel like a victim. She helped me reshape my view of the world so that I can feel so grateful for life. If searching for greater meaning and purpose in life is something that appeals to you, I have no hesitation in recommending Rachel to help you on your way. What's changed for me since working with Rachel is that I've been to Guatemala to do a Moon course. This is a one-month retreat that focuses on reconnecting with higher states of consciousness. It involves yoga meditation, fasting, silence and workshops on tarot astrology, pranayama breathing, the Kabballah and Kyballion. I am in no doubt that there are higher dimensions we can enter, with will-power, patience, self-control and wisdom. I feel I am responsible for making my world brighter. I see spiritual growth as my priority, after all, spirit is the one thing we take with us when we die. I feel different about this now after working with Rachel because I am more certain of it.

Lucy Noble – Business Owner

I love doing *Rise and Shine*. When I signed up originally, I was concerned that it would take a lot of effort to turn up twice a day, but once I had rearranged my schedule a little, I found little effort was required and I look forward to each session. Since starting, I understand more about what is important to me and how I need to prioritise those things without guilt. I feel much happier and everyone around me has noticed this change.

It is nearly a year since I started. There have been short breaks when I have been very busy, but I always come back to it knowing that when I am committed, my life flows easily and effortlessly, regardless of any challenges I face. This programme has been life changing for me. Paying close attention to my emotions every day and knowing that I can change how I feel is amazing. It has positively affected all aspects of my life. Working with Rachel is a joy. I appreciate the energy and care she brings to all the sessions and I feel deeply supported.

Leona Ralph – Medical Herbalist

Working with Rachel provides a great lesson in who you are, who you can be and how to get there.

Jo Powles-Brown – Coach, Healer and Sophrologist

I have been working with Rachel Jenkins since May 2017, incorporating the *Rise and Shine* practise in my life and it has really been amazing.

Things have happened that I had actually "created" in my morning goal setting *Rise and Shine* meditation. Some things did not happen immediately, but slowly and surely. I have ridden some storms knowing that someone is invisibly behind me, has my back as it were. Rachel is a genuine and caring person, who gently keeps the pressure on! It has been enlightening and on a good few occasions, a challenging experience!

I would highly recommend working with Rachel Jenkins on the *Rise and Shine* programme, for anyone interested in forwarding their lives, and setting and achieving their goals in a persistent and creative manner- using meditation as the entry point.

Jerome Flynn - Actor

The *Rise and Shine* programme has been a wonderful journey of reconnection to the heart. It has given me simple tools that greatly help me to call in (and create) the way I want to live and feel each day.

Through daily practice, the rewiring of thought and behavioural patterns help to bring me back to the truth- that joyful engagement with life really is in my hands, and that the transformative power of self-love is always available to us, if we will just let it in. Wonderful stuff Rachel, thank you!

Emma Lynn – Singer/Song Writer

Rachel is incredibly intuitive which creates a safe space, because she taps into things that you don't necessarily say out loud, and that is very empowering. It creates a lot of room to be honest in discussions.

What it also means is that all energies are reflected back to you in a really exciting way, because I feel that she is very expressive and very honest, so I would say that working with Rachel allows for a safe and exciting place, where you really feel heard and understood.

The biggest thing that has changed for me since learning and incorporating the *Rise and Shine* practise is the ownership I feel of my life and my days. I have suffered for a long time with depression and anxiety. It was very overwhelming for me to try and develop strategic plans for my days, but because the *Rise and Shine* practise is very fun (and can be a light hearted, visual practise), I feel like it takes away the overwhelm, and creates a safe and relaxed space. I feel it really is getting to the core of what I want, and that makes it easy to keep coming back to those goals that you set at the beginning of the day. It also creates a lovely supportive atmosphere for the day instead of an atmosphere of overwhelm or fear.

Also, because you are setting up your day very intentionally- and it's such a calming and soothing practice- I really feel that it does overcome the initial fatigue and dark thoughts that are present when you are in a bad space of depression. It transforms them into a real-life energy, so that your days begin to flow more outwards instead of being so introspective and heavy.

People who would benefit from working with Rachel and learning *Rise and Shine* are definitely people with depression and anxiety. It is such a powerful practise to transform the energy of your life and, I would say people going through confusing times (such as times of transition) would really benefit too. It is just such a lovely way of anchoring into what you really want to get out of each day, and slowly day by day knowing that you have created something new and exciting.

Christopher Howard - Founder of Wealth & Achievement Academy

The *Rise & Shine* Programme has the capacity to revolutionise the Mental Health system, globally.

Belinda Ray – 'The Passionate Pilgrim'

Thanks to invaluable help from Rachel's expertise and practical magic toolbox, I love how I am now creating a new positive force field in my life. I am now cultivating the habits of honouring myself and getting to know how to work with my highest potential. That's energising.

A big change to my life has been spotting more of the sneaky 'sabotage' tricks of my mind, and creating simple strategies to overcome them. I now feel more compassion and acceptance for myself and others with all our foibles. That's more inner peace.

My childlike creativity is beginning to flow again. It is wonderful! When you do this practice daily, you're actively building the muscles of vision, self-belief, and effective strategies to keep you moving towards your goals. It's a feeling of buoyancy and real resilience! You're preparing for whatever it takes to create the life you were born to live. If you feel you need to radically change your life… to start really living from your heart and soul, to access your own inner guidance, to get more creative and trusting in life… just do it. Sign up. And DO IT. You won't be disappointed.

Rachel is definitely onto something powerfully transformative for the common good here. I'm deeply grateful and inspired by her big-hearted commitment to the 'vision in action' and to sharing this practice far and wide. The world needs much more of this. For life's sake, come let's *Rise and Shine* together!

Andrea Evans - Clinical Consultant Psychologist

Since working with Rachel, positive energy has flowed into my whole life for good; at work, in friendships, business and life generally. I loved the strong women, the cheerleading energy and support, the one-to-one wisdom from Rachel and the group sessions. I loved learning, growing and re-discovering my passion.

I have a completely different mind-set: positive, growing, exciting, soaring! I feel like a different person. The biggest changes that have happened since I started *Perform* are an earlier bed-time, better diet, maintained weight-loss and I function better in the daytime. I have a better grip over my budget and now have a new car, which six months ago just wasn't even a possibility.

Working with Rachel is life-changing.

Amanda Short – Virtual Assistant

I reached out to Rachel during a crisis in my life. She invited me to take part in her programme so that I could gain some control back over my life. This proved to be an invaluable experience and helped pull me out of a situation that felt helpless. I also formed a good relationship with Rachel.

When I did the *Rise and Shine* programme, I found a purpose and a focus outside of my crisis which helped change my mindset and made me feel worthy of success - a feeling which is now deeply embedded in my soul. One of my greatest realisations during *Rise and Shine* was that my value is not determined by another person's failure to see my worth. I restored my self-belief and launched my own business in 2018, which is growing from strength to strength. Rachel is laser-focused and has unshakeable belief in her own ability to help people; something I'm happy to say I now share. *Rise and Shine* is her tool, and she uses it to great effect to do just that. Anyone in a situation which no longer serves them can benefit from it, because it is literally like a guiding light pointing you in the direction that you (already know) you should go, and then helping you along that path."

I think it's important to mention what triggered my awakening. I recall constantly hitting a 'sticking point' with my business. It would only get so far, only so good, so profitable and I always seemed to hit a plateau that I would never seem to be able to push past. There was something stopping me that I could not put my finger on. I came to Rachel to help me figure out what was preventing me from taking the next step forward. I was getting divorced and as much as I knew I was in pain, I wasn't fully aware of the full effects.

By becoming more self-aware of my environment and how it had been affecting me - I started to build this barrier to protect myself. I didn't begin blocking people – rather, just became self-aware of who I am, and that other people are not a part of me nor an extension of me. I was fully in control and if I chose to stay in that environment then I could only expect more of the same. I didn't want that: I wanted a healthy life, to be full of energy, happy, successful... and that would only happen by focusing on myself.

The business is now thriving to a point where I have tripled my turnover since I first began this journey, and it is about to double again over the next twelve months. I look back to where I was before I made that leap of self-discovery and recognise that I was on the verge of a mental breakdown, where I would have been of no help to my son, my family or my business. If I was to give any advice to my younger self, it would be that when going through separation and divorce, it takes three years to emotionally start rebuilding, and five to financially get past that situation. The breakup takes less time if you let go of all the anger, the hate, the negativity, the self-deprecating, limiting beliefs about yourself, who you can be, your possibilities, and you learn to love yourself again.

Believe in yourself and that anything is possible, then the world is your oyster. There is one quote that I remember hearing years ago from a very well know business man, Richard Branson; he made a comment that when he used to go for things, (for contracts etc) he used to say *yes*. He figured he could do it and then afterwards, would figure out how. That always used to resonate with me throughout my life, and once I started accepting that it was coming into my awareness for a reason, I began applying it- go for it, do it, figure out how later along the journey of where you want to go, because that's the fun part.

I can look back and understand now that by coming to Rachel and seeking her assistance with one small aspect of my life, it helped me find the door, gave me the tools on how to open the door and then it was ME that took myself through it.

So, my breakthrough is me getting through that door, becoming self-aware, self-managing and in the nick of time too, because I am a shadow of my former self. I am scared to think where I would be had I not had that breakthrough and taken the steps into self-awareness, the secret to life and the freedom that it brings.

During the 7-day Reset *Rise and Shine* programme, I earned more in that one month than I had done since leaving regular employment as a Secondary School teacher, two-years earlier.

I was getting up and spending the time looking into my heart and doing Rachel's meditations – there was one I really connected with I think – when you do the staircase down from the head to the heart and I felt that during that time, you are saying to the universe, 'I am worth it, I am worth investing in myself instead of constantly investing in other people' – what I mean is putting *myself* first, instead of thinking, "Oh I must do this. I've got to do that, I must make sure that person has been helped to the best of my ability" ...actually all I need to do is help myself to the best of my ability.

What I have learnt from doing the R&S programme is that I AM the most important thing – I must always prioritise myself above all else, which sounds hard when you are trying to lead a practical life style. However, in those moments when you put yourself first, you are giving so much back to everybody else and the universe; that's when you begin to make big leaps and it can be in the forms of money, realisations, any of those things you shift. It's because I love myself that that I am prepared to give myself that time.

In June 2018, when I participated in the *Rise and Shine* programme, I gave myself even more time to connect in with 'me' so that I felt more aligned with everything I was doing on a daily basis. It is energy input and output, so when you are able to focus with the R&S programme, you look at how you want you feel at the beginning of the day and how you want to feel at the end of the day, so if you are giving out and putting back (in the present) every single moment, then you are going to feel abundance and this will show up as financial success, just as it did for me. If you have been working on the inner "stuff", it has to balance on for outer "stuff" too!

I was shown through working on myself though the *Rise and Shine* programme over a dedicated 21-day period, how quickly you can create in your physical world, what you want. I always maintain that you 100% create your own reality, so when you are in the best emotional state (that empowers you), unexpected fortunes can happen because you are in a pure balanced state. During the *Rise and Shine* programme, I closed financial deals at a higher level than before even though I hadn't been focusing on that. I had been focusing on my well-being! So, there is a link between your inner well-being and you outer well-being, whether that be physical or financial.

Jenna Kitchingham - Spirit Voyager, Researcher and Writer

At the start of my journey with Rachel and the *Rise and Shine* programme, I didn't have faith in myself and I was not even aware of it! I had long forgotten what having faith in myself felt like. To become aware that I was lacking faith, I first needed to stop, look inward and outline what I truly wanted, rather than moving on the treadmill of life.

Starting the *Rise and Shine* programme with Rachel in May 2016 began this inward journey to my heart, which I had been ignoring for a long time. I had forgotten my inner magic. Every time I looked inside myself, I was getting physically ill. I experienced chest infections that would last a couple of weeks and I couldn't shift them, even though I was perfectly healthy in all my other aspects, but my heart knew exactly what was needed, whilst my mind had no idea.

Through the *Rise and Shine* masterclasses with Rachel I started to see glimpses of the person I used to be in my late teens, who was absolutely unstoppable and had the capability to manifest everything I wished for... I had never doubted that ability.

Over the next ten years, I lost the connection with this inner power, by working in male dominated property industries and picking relationships with people who put me down through their words and actions.

I even married someone who did not support my dreams. I was married when I started the *Rise and Shine* programme. I have now learnt that no-one can do anything to me without my permission. It was time to take responsibility for how I had allowed myself to be treated. This was the hardest step.

Through the *Rise and Shine* programme, I was able to take the steps gently, and in a heart focused way with childlike celebration, something I had not given myself for a very long time. Up until then, I had become a perfectionist in all my endeavours and spoke to myself very badly. It was hard to admit that I was accountable but as challenging as that was, this was the freedom step to empowering myself and re-gaining my faith.

I had searched outwardly in so many areas including yoga training, reiki healing and other healing modalities, even academic achievements. Strangely, no-one ever taught me that all the magic lives inside me. It's true what they say, that you can try to change for years, but it all happens in a single moment of realisation. We must however be gentle on ourselves, because the engrained patterns of our ego mind take time and gentle encouragement to catch up to the realisation that all the magic lies within.

I shifted very quickly over the space of about three months, where it felt like the cage had been lifted and my life once more had infinite possibilities.

We really are the creators of our own destiny.

I thank Rachel for opening the doorway to my heart, so I can now live my life where I feel free and deeply happy within every situation and decision I make.

Shion Buschner- Acupuncturist, Sacred Sound Healer

In 2016, I had a major breakdown after the death of my late husband which landed me in a coma and at death's door, with all my organs failing. By divine intervention, I was given a second chance, which was when I met Rachel. I was in desperate need of turning my life around, and needed to rebuild my life.

When I came out of my coma, I was going through the motions of being a functioning human and maybe even appearing as one, but I myself felt far from that; on the contrary, getting through the day often resembled a desperate state of affairs. I couldn't speak, stand up or make sense of anything. I felt totally disconnected and was seriously failing to find much meaning, or how to carry on.

I remember clearly explaining to Rachel in my initial interview for the *Rise and Shine* practice, that it was a matter of life or death- whether I would be able to get a grip and turn my life around. Rachel gave me the tools to do so. I reclaimed my life, found exquisite happiness, greater inner fulfilment and a whole new world opened up, (which at one point I thought was for me, totally and utterly out of reach.)

The most important thing to say is that I have a different sense of myself these days; a sense of 'me' that I didn't used to have. I would say when you work with Rachel, you are really working with intention, and this is really at the heart of my daily practise: setting intentions, (you can also call it 'prayer', and really for me that has really meant to follow the highest guidance of spirit.)

My focus and my happiness come from living an awakened life. That means being deeply connected to source and the gifts that come are mind-blowing. It's difficult to put into words.

My relationships are much better these days and I know that it is a result of my relationship with myself. What is really important to say here is that historically, I always thought I was in charge and I was responsible. I have realised that I did not allow for spirit or God. I have not allowed myself to be held by spirit before, mainly because I had a belief system that I was deeply unlovable. Lots has now changed with the work I have done with Rachel over the last year, and some other people in a healing capacity also. What I find is that embracing fully where we are, right here, right now, and in connecting with spirit's guidance... true healing can happen. In my experience, Rachel's work of aligning with heaven and earth, provides that daily platform. Only from THAT place, can we make plans and decisions that have a chance to lead us into our place of happiness.

Possibilities beyond my wildest dreams are now manifesting on a daily basis. Also, I no longer attempt to change situations (which at face value seem undesirable). In other words, I have discovered that when I trust in the universe, I become aware of a higher intelligence that seems to be at work, and manifest possibilities that my own ego mind could never have considered in the first place.

Rachel's work shifts mountains. My gratitude is immense.

If you would like to share your own story, contact Rachel or join *Rise and Shine*, please visit:
www.racheljenkins.online

Being at home with yourself is the key
Let it all go and decide to be free,
Always Trust Love and Live *your* truth
Peace every day is living proof.

With Love,

Rachel

37001799R00101

Printed in Poland
by Amazon Fulfillment
Poland Sp. z o.o., Wrocław